Sewing Doesn't Have to be a Mystery

Answers to Many Sewing and Serging Machine Challenges

Everyone has at least one button hanging by a thread.

Authored & Photographed by Stephnie Clark
With Illustrations by the Author and Donna Akiona

AuthorHouse™
1663 Liberty Drive, Suite 200
Bloomington, IN 47403
www.authorhouse.com
Phone: 1-800-839-8640

First published by AuthorHouse 8/5/2009

ISBN: 978-1-4389-4031-1 (sc)

Printed in the United States of America
Bloomington, Indiana

This book is printed on acid-free paper.

The information in this book is presented in good faith, but no results are guaranteed. Since the author has no control over the circumstances under which the instructions and named products are applied, the author disclaims any liability from results. Also, this book in no way covers all a seamstress needs to know. It would take a huge cumbersome book to include everything. The purpose of this book is to get you on the "right" tract making your sewing experience worth while. I suggest you take sewing lessons from a knowledgeable sewing instructor; she will enhance the books illustrations and instructions.
Simply put: sew for the fun of it!

Acknowledgments

It gives me great pleasure to thank those unsung hero's walking around with buttons hanging by a thread, seams gapping open and especially those with partially fallen hems. Thank you for inspiring me to write this book.

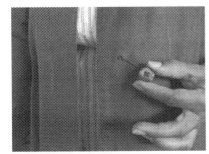 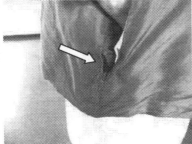 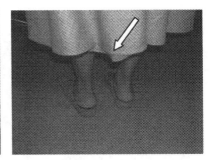

A special thanks goes to the following: Rosie Verdugo for her sewing machine needle tip; Carolyn Curtis author of the <u>Kids Can Sew Program</u>; Librarians Anna McElroy and Grace Francisco for their undying support, plus Gene Baird, Shannon Lin, Vanessa Lebron, and Joe Pergolizzi at the Mission Branch Oceanside Library computer lab "geeks" who helped me with the confounded computer; my students of which this book would not have been written; Antique Sewing Machines, January 12, 2007, for the use of the antique sewing machine pictures; Sue Mezera of Quilter's Paradise in Escondido, California, for being gracious enough to pose for me without warning; Rita Campo Griggs, Palomar College Interior Design and Fashion Department, San Marcos, California, for loaning her book on fashion shows, and most of all my friend, Candace Cochrane, for her tireless encouragement. Also many thanks goes to my attendees at the book reading and luncheon: Noreen Ring for playing the devils advocate; Shannon Lin always cheerful and ready to help; Danielle Motherhead we cut yardage together at Hancock Fabric; Candace Cochrane we sold sewing machines together; Hannah Elliott, Rosie Kansky, and Alicia Flaker (just three of my loyal students) all of which put me through the literary wringer and made me a better writer. Nancysnotions.com has been my most favorite source for wonderful sewing and quilting products we sewers need.

Introduction

How to use this book!

There are many problems people experience while learning to sew. All beginning students invariably repeat the same tendencies making their sewing experience quite difficult. Too often the potential seamstress will opt out in favor of ready made. Stephnie's observation of her students in class and private lessons prompted her to identify the common and often daunting tendencies. She addressed about 95 of these tendencies, wrote down her solutions the way she described them in her classes and finally compiled them in book form and named it <u>Sewing Doesn't Have to be a Mystery, Answers to Many Sewing and Serging Challenges</u>.

Many times as you read this book you will come across the phrase "Take a moment before you…". That moment you take will save you wasted time ripping, unnecessary trips to the repair shop, broken needles, emergency stops at the fabric store and the frustration of it all. (Well, who needs an excuse to go shopping at the fabric store?)

Of the greatest importance is the Thread Jamb tendency. You will find them in Section 5. The book offers this one to help you understand a simple rule. You can solve just about any Thread Jamb provided you know what you did to cause it. By following these tendencies and their solutions you will be developing good sewing habits while creating an environment of many happy and productive hours at the sewing machine.

Stephnie included a few mending tasks with the intention of showing you, the reader, how to fix them; proficiently. [Section V, Tendencies 17-1 through 17-4] "Replacing a button, closing up a seam, and what? You stapled your hem? You know who you are" she said as she narrowed her eyes. "Don't the staples catch on your stockings?" But seriously, getting your mending basket emptied using your new sewing skills and placing these items back into your closet and linen drawers will grant you the satisfaction of a job well done. Plus this will save you time and money because you didn't have to drive to the gas station and gas up for a hefty price and then to the department store to buy more clothes. Same goes for the window treatments: have you prices them lately? How smart you are when you sew!

Stephnie has set up the following drawings, photos and explanations to help you while learning tasks you didn't even know you and your sewing machine could perform. And do it with ease. But most importantly she pokes fun at the irritating and often amusing tendencies. Also there is a section on reading pattern envelopes. Stephnie mentions many tools, "toys" as we call them, to help you while sewing. All these instructions may appear overwhelming in the beginning. But, if you repeat these tasks over and over they will become good habits. You know, like good posture! Use <u>Sewing Doesn't Have to be a Mystery</u> as a reference book when you get bogged down.

A special note from Stephnie about buying a sewing machine:

When you get ready to purchase your first sewing machine or up-date your existing machine, I recommend you take a few sewing lessons. Some sewing teachers have machines for their beginning students to use. A three month course can make a difference. These sewing lessons will show you where your newly developed talents can take you. If your sewing teacher understands the difference between the various sewing machine brands, she will be a good source to help you purchase your machine, <u>one that will grow with you</u>. My history of selling several different sewing machine brands (ex. Baby Lock, Elna, Singer, Viking, and White) and helped students with other sewing machines, such as Bernina, has enhanced my ability to assist people in choosing the perfect machine for them. All the students that have gone through my program are still happy with their sewing machine choices.

Cost <u>is</u> a factor! However, please don't allow cost to be the most important one. When purchasing a sewing machine, consider it an investment in your future sewing projects: something like college but with a much lower price tag. Choose wisely! It can be discouraging if you should outgrow your sewing machine while you are learning to sew. A good one will run from $400 on up to many thousands of dollars. MANY THOUSANDS OF DOLLARS? That is enough to scare anyone into purchasing a *cheap sewing machine*. I beseech you to resist the temptation, if you can. Buying from discount stores or, heaven for bid, on the internet can be a risky and expensive endeavor. Also beware of deceptive pricing: $79 for a machine is a gamble you do not want to take. One alternative: while taking your sewing lessons, seek out a sewing machine shop that offers a lay-a-way plan and <u>"just do it"</u>.

Keep in mind one simple rule: Everyone needs to do mending. Life happens, repair it! For some people, all you will need is a sewing machine that can: 1) sew a decent hem; 2) close up any seams that come undone; and 3) lower or cover the feed teeth to sew on a button. Remember: <u>sewing fine garments and complicated home decor is not for everyone</u>. It can be very tedious and time consuming work. Your first group of sewing lessons will be a great help in deciding how far you want to take your sewing experience. But, if you are up for a challenge, you will discover sewing is extremely satisfying.

I recommend no more than two lessons per week: trust me you will become overwhelmed. More importantly try not to have an unrealistic dead-line for your sewing projects. Mistakes abound when you are in a hurry.

[Where I have described special sewing tools in the text, I printed the names in *Italics*. Example: *seam ripper*. *Singer Co.* makes a great *seam ripper* with a curved handle.]

<u>I trust you will have many happy socializing hours in your sewing classes.</u>

Articles, famous quotes & Manufacturers:
Nancy's Notion on-line, a great place to shop

Sewing/Serging Machine companies:
>*Bernina* has uniquely designed feet and the system for changing them.
>*Singer* produces many fine and useful sewing tools, "toys".
>Upper line *Viking* sewing machines are still made in Sweden.
>*Baby Lock* serging machines thread with a poof of air.
>The *Pffaf* sewing machine has always had its own built-in Walking foot.
>*Elna* sewing and pressing products are available through reputable dealers.

Gingher pinking scissors, Threads Magazine #131, page 14.

Pattern Companies:
>*New look* are mostly easy and priced much lower than other patterns.
>V*ogue*: my favorite.
>*Burda* have intricately designed features for advanced seamstresses.
>Ann Person Collectibles, students made and modeled in my Summer Fashion Show
>Simplicity is always reliable and can be found at Wal-Mart for a little less money.

"…and the stitches "bed down" to create inconspicuous seams" Taken from the <u>Complete Guide to Sewing</u> Readers Digest, 1995, page 12

"*Please make a note of it.*" Information Operator

"*Oh, Bother*" said Winnie the Pooh

"The *Ugly Side* and The *Pretty Side*" <u>Kids Can Sew Program </u>by Carolyn Curtis

"*Just do it*" from Nike shoes

"*Huston, we have a problem!*" said the astronaut out in space.

<u>Threads Magazine</u>: *Silk Thread* Ad's

"Wash your stash" by Judith Newham appeared in <u>Threads Magazine</u> #118, page 38
<u>Titanic Shipwrecks and Sunken Treasures</u>, Page 93 of the glossary

"Are you looking directly at the foot? No cheating! Look straight ahead", from the teacher's manual at Sew Pros, by Janie Tuledge.

Stores where I taught sewing: Yardage Town, Vista and Encinitas; Hancock Fabrics, Oceanside; JoAnn Fabrics/Crafts, Oceanside; Sew Pros Sewing and Vacuum, Oceanside; House of Fabric, Seattle.

Table of Contents

Section I
Perfection

Section II
Pins, Fabric, Notions, Patterns, Scissors

The general basics are described in detail including pins and needles, handy bobs, scissor posture, help with some fabric lingo, and making sense of what the different parts of the pattern are used for.

Section III
Machine Parts and preparing the machine for sewing

Recognizing basic areas of the machine and the feet (not the ones you stand on) that are similar to the different manufacturers is our next topic: plus interesting and informative stuff about your PowerCord/FootPeddle (PC/FP).

Section IV

Posture, Irons, Hand Sewing

Posture! You sound like my mother. Iron! Who has one these days? There are ways to replace a button or re-hem a skirt with all kinds of fancy and expensive gadgets to assist you but nothing can replace the old-fashion needle and thread.

Section V

Sewing Techniques

There are several areas to concentrate on when preparing to sew with your machines. Strange and unwanted things happen. We will take a look at several of these sewing problems. This section will help you understand how to develop your eye-hand-foot coordination as you study this book and through your practice. As far as Thread Jambs are concerned, your reward awaits you in chapter 16.

Section VI

Computerized Machines and Patterns

Wow! The sewing industry has been listening to our concerns and they have improved the overall operation of the machines as well as the irksome time and effort wasters. We will deal with areas to look for on the pattern envelope to help you be a proficient shopper. Yes! And the pattern instructions are exasperating: but help is on its way.

Appendix

Sewing doesn't have to be a mystery!

Notes:

Section I

Perfection

Note: As a beginning sewer

I encourage you to follow this first entry

until you have more confidence

in your ability to sew

comfortably.

1-1)Tendency…Beginning sewers and perfection do not mix. Relax and have fun while learning to sew. Perfection is in the future.

The Problem…I am very serious about this one. In the beginning…

Bulletin: New sewers do not need to be perfect!

Sewing perfectly is not important at this stage of your sewing experience. Attempting to be perfect in the beginning will become frustrating and you may decide sewing is not for you. Remember, ripping is discouraging to any sewer, especially when you are just starting to learn.

To Clarify…..Please relax, and have fun. *Take a sewing class.* It is beneficial and more fun than trying to learn on your own. But, when you advance to tailoring, well, <u>that</u> is a different story.

Oh Bother! I forgot the pins and the tape measure. Check list: pattern; all fabrics required; measuring tape or ruler; cutting tools (bent-handled scissors or rotary cutter); pins; instruction sheet and cutting board or matt and any trims. Now you are ready to cut.

Section II

Pins

Notions

Patterns

Fabrics

Scissors

My little functioning sculpture!

#2   I'm on Pins and Needles

2-1   Sewing over pins.

2-2   Pins sticking over the edge of the pattern.

2-3   Picking up the pattern/fabric while pinning them together.

2-4   Taking up too much fabric while pinning, the "big stitch"

2-5   The pins with the colorful ball heads are pretty, but…

2-6   Beginning sewers push the head of the pin as far as it will go.

2-7   What is the purpose of pinning the pattern to the fabric?

2-8   When was the last time you changed your sewing machine needle?

2-9   Needles, which one do I use? Can't I just use the same one?

2-10   Why do I have long stitches and short stitches?

2-11   The seam is finished but the fabric will not budge from my machine.

2-12   It is REALY scary breaking a needle on a computer sewing machine.

Photo 2-1

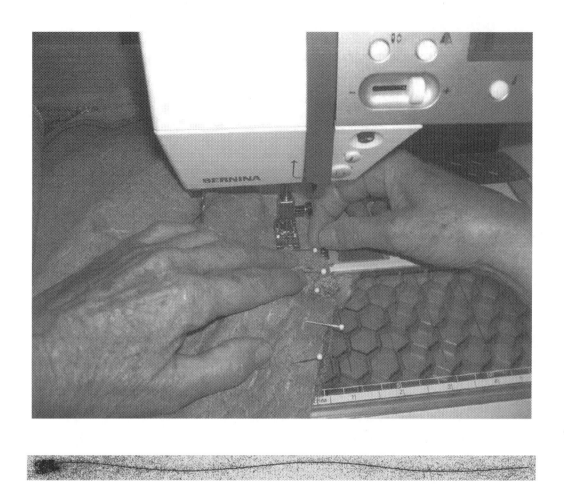

Drawing 2-2

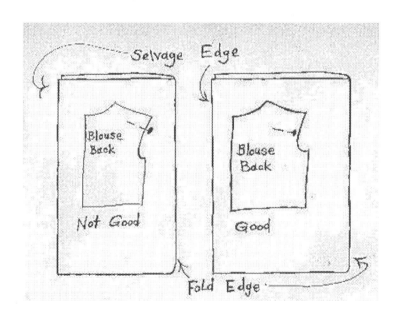

2-1) Tendency….My mother sewed over pins. What was good for her is good enough for me. Or: maybe not.

The Problem…..If this attitude is taken to the serging machine, pins can cause extensive damage if the pin reaches the blade. A chipped blade, a broken pin, needle "heaven", a damaged hook, personal injury, and dare I say damaged fabric comes to mind. Any one of these things can happen when sewing over pins. Raising havoc with the machines timing and alignment will send you and your machine to the technician. Oh No! Not to mention the stitches will fall apart and you will have to sew the seam again. "Oh Bother" said Pooh. I remember one time I was mindlessly sewing along when, before I could pull the pin, the needle came *crashing* down and smack dab on the needle. It snapped and sent the broken piece careening upwards. What a scare when I realized the needle had grazed my forehead.

To Clarify….From that day forward, I consciously remove the pins before they reach the foot. But that does not mean to remove the pins too soon. The pins are there to hold your fabric pieces together until they disappear under the foot. Once the pin reaches the foot, simply grab the pin head and pull it out of the fabric. (Photo 2-1) The needle screw, as it moves downward, can be a source of tear jerking pain if you do not get your fingers out of the way. I have trained my fingers to grab the head of the pin with my thumb nail. I angle my thumb parallel to the machines surface. This method is especially effective when sewing the crown section of a sleeve. You see, I place a bazillion pins to ease in the fullness. Oops! This is an entirely different subject. Until you develop the eye-hand-foot coordination, stop the machine before pulling out the pin. The Serging Machine blade can fall pray to sever damage. Some serging machines require a technician to replace the blade(s) costing you tons of dollars you could be spending on that special trim you had your eye on. For pin placement using your serging machine see Photo 8-4 page 77.

~~~~~ **D O   N O T   S E W   O V E R   P I N S !** ~~~~~

2-2)Tendency….Everyone new to sewing places the pins to close to the cutting line of the pattern and allows the pins to extend beyond the pattern edge.

The Problem….This is bad for two reasons: One, as you cut out the fabric you may cut the pin and knick the scissors. Remember, scissor sharpening service is at lease $8 a pair. Two, if you left up the fabric/pattern to cut under the pin you will cut a really odd edge compromising the construction of your sewing project. Example: pinning the bodice to the sleeve will result in one piece extending beyond the other. Seams will not come together and the blouse will be uncomfortable to wear not to mention how funny the garment will look. If that's the look you want, well!

To Clarify….I recommend pinning about ¾" inside the cutting line of the pattern so that the head of the pin will be with-in the tissue pattern cutting line. (Drawing 2-2) As you pin, keep moving the pin farther and farther away from the cutting line of the pattern. I tell my students: "Move your pin in, more, still more." After a while they develop instinctively the eye-hand coordination to know how far from the cutting edge to start pushing the pin into the pattern/fabric. With practice so can you!

Photo 2-3a

Much better

Photo 2-3b

So-So

Drawing 2-4

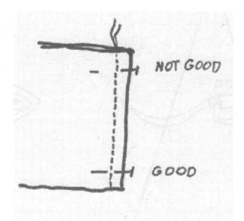

[The sewn seam over the pins is purely for demonstration, only. Remember: pull pins out before sewing over them.]

Photo 2-4

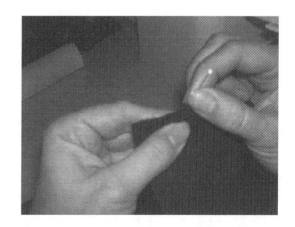

2-3) Tendency…I see beginning and advanced students picking up the pattern/fabric when pinning. (Photo 2-3a)

The Problem… The pattern/fabric can shift in your hand while pinning.

To Clarify.....When pinning pattern to fabric, you need to make sure the layers do not slide around. To begin with, place your pattern/fabric flat on the table. Rest one hand on top next to where you are going to pin. With the other hand holding the head of the pin, slide the pin (using a slight sawing motion) until it touches the table. Now you know you have gone through all the layers. [I suggest using a *cardboard cutting board* on your good dining table to protect your fine table surface. Another surface to place this cutting board on is your bed: this way you will not pin to the bedspread. The board is folded *accordion style* for easy storage.] Lift up pattern/fabric <u>slightly</u>, using the pin. (Photo 2-3a) Slide the pin forward. It is better to make as tiny a "stitch" as the layers will allow. Exit the pattern/fabric past your finger on your other hand. This one will take some practice, but it is worth it. Position your finger so you won't get pricked and draw blood. For heavier fabrics you will have to make a "big stitch". [This is where the *quilting or long silk glass head pins* come in handy.] Do not leave the pattern/fabric bunched up. Center the pin in this "stitch" you just made through all the layers. This will flatten the area making it smooth and allowing you to cut more accurately. A moment taken here will save you from having to pin again, or worse make a poor cut.

2-4)Tendency…Too many sewers bunch up fabric with the pin or do not pin at all when preparing for sewing by hand or on the sewing machine.

The Problem.....The action of sticking the pin straight down into the fabric compels you to take a "big stitch" with the pin. Conversely, if you should opt to sew a straight or curved seam without pinning you run the risk of sewing the seam crooked and could stretch the fabric out of shape.

To Clarify…...Pinning correctly can make a big difference in the finished product. To prepare fabric for the machine, steer clear of pinning the fabric if it is resting on the table. You need to have complete control of the layers at that precise spot as you pin: unlike pinning fabric to pattern where you need the table to steady everything. A "tiny stitch" holds the layers together more efficiently. This pinning indicates <u>exactly</u> where the seam is to be sewn. I hold the fabric precisely where the seam is to be sewn; a standard seam allowance is 5/8" in from the cut edge. Instead of sticking the pin straight down, I take the pin and slide it between my thumb and fabric. (Photo 2-4) At this point the pin is almost flat to the fabric. Slide the pin just until you feel the point on you finger. {Draw no blood today. But, for heaven sakes, if you do prick your finger put a *bandage* on it right away to keep from bleeding on your sewing project. I keep some in my *sewing basket* for such emergencies.} Before sliding the pin any further, immediately ease it back to the top of the fabric. This "*tiny stitch*" will control a much wider area then a "big stitch". (Drawing 2-4) Notice the head of the pin sticks out <u>beyond</u> the fabric edge making it easily accessible when pulling the pin out of the fabric as it approaches the foot. Now I know I have placed the pin faithfully where I am going to sew. It is not necessary to pin too close, about 5 – 8 inches part is plenty for a straight seam. Of course you will need to pin more often in a curve. Practice this and you will find your sewing becomes less stressful.

Drawing 2-5

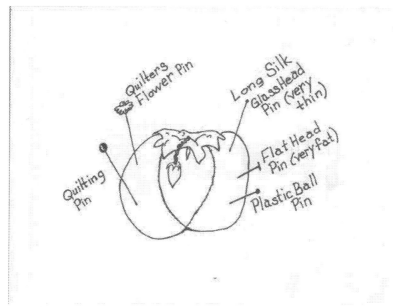

I use the *Flat Head silk pins* as a backup because the head is rather difficult for me to grasp.

Photo 2-5

There are many more packages of pins available at the stores and on-line.

2-5)Tendency…The pins with the colored plastic ball heads are pretty, but….

The Problem…Not all pins are equal. I know they are pretty, but, very often there is no pointy-end or the colored ball falls off. "Oh, Bother" said Winnie the Pooh. There is a huge assortment of pins on the market that do specific tasks. However, most of them are not suitable for sewing. Example: the fat pins, I call them nails; really short pins, for using with sequins; the pretty pearl colored ball pins which fall off; and the list goes on. (Photo 2-5)

To Clarify……..I recommend purchasing the *long silk flat head or glass head pins.* (Drawing 2-5) They slide in and out with ease. And, the glass head ball does not come off. While teaching classes at *Yardage Town* store, I was helping a student pin her fabric (it had a painted design on the fabric and was very tough to get the pin through the fabric). Well, as I struggled, the plastic pearlized ball came off penetrating that end of the pin into my finger. Man! Did that Hurt! After we bandaged my finger, she immediately bought the *long silk glass head pins.* I do not mind shedding a little blood if it helps beginning sewers find the process of sewing to be extremely satisfying and not harmful to their health.

Drawing 2-6

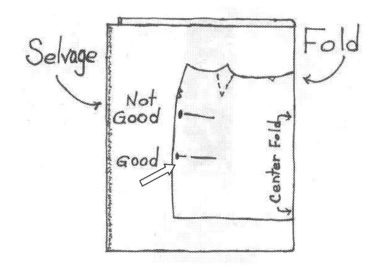

Drawing 2-7

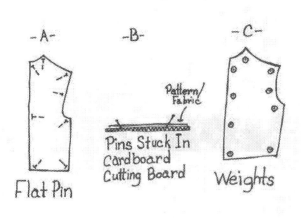

2-6)Tendency…When pinning the fabric for cutting and sewing, beginning sewers will push the head of the pin as far as it will go. Not good.

The Problem….You will make a rough cut. This is unsatisfactory because that piece may not fit to the adjoining piece as you pin them together, example: front and back blouse side seams, they will be uneven. Also, the chance of sewing over pins is too risky. And you know how bad sewing over pins can be. (Tendency 2-1, page 8)

To Clarify…….When you pin the pattern to the fabric or prepare it for sewing, the pin needs to enter and exit the fabric twice. I call this a "stitch". This stitch should be in the middle of the pin. (Drawing 2-6: the arrow shows the "tiny stitch" and unfortunately my drawing is a bit off center, "Oh Dear") I have actually had students stick the pin in the fabric and not bring it back up through the fabric. Of course the pin falls out, hopefully not in the carpet. I find *Long Glass Head Silk pins* are best for garment sewing. With heavy fabric it is difficult to pin with a "*tiny stitch*", the fabric taking up the whole pin. Loosely woven fabrics can be a problem as well. The *Long Quilters pins* with the flat flower head (Drawing 2-5, page 11) work satisfactorily. A word of caution: I have seen mangled pins that did not survive their plight under the foot. This is not good for the foot or the feed dogs, (teeth) not to mention the fabric and needle you just damaged. In this situation, I encourage beginners to sew slowly: allow enough time to take their foot off the foot peddle just as the pin reaches the foot so they can pull out the pin, effortlessly.

2-7) Tendency…"What is the purpose of pinning the pattern to the fabric?" "I do not have time for this extra work,"

The Problem….When cutting, if you only place your hand on the pattern and the two layers of fabric as they rest on the table, chances are the layers will slide around making it difficult to cut. When you try to sew the pieces together they probably will not line up causing your sewing project to look pretty weird. Oh! And by the way, I do not recommend sewing when you are pressed for time. You know the phrase: "The faster I go the bee hinder I get?" It is not worth the agony if your sewing project comes out badly.

To Clarify……..There are three ways to "pin down" your pattern: Drawing 2-7a, pinning flat to the pattern and fabric; Drawing 2-7b is a cross section, sticking the pins perpendicular into a *cardboard cutting board* (see the pins how they are angled away from each other, this holds pattern and fabric together without shifting); or Drawing 2-7c, uses *weights* to "pin down" the pattern to the fabric. There is a long thin worm like weight that works well when using a rotary cutter. Be sure you use a special *cutting matt* when using the *rotary cutter*. The matt has a special surface that heals it's self as the blade moves across. There are several sizes' available in the quilting department of your fabric store. Check out the *large matt* for your rectangle cutting table. Quilters really like this size. [Note: When working with velvet and stain it is better to pin in the SA (seam allowance) area. I recommend saving these fabrics until you reach the advanced stage of your sewing lessons.]

Drawing 2-8

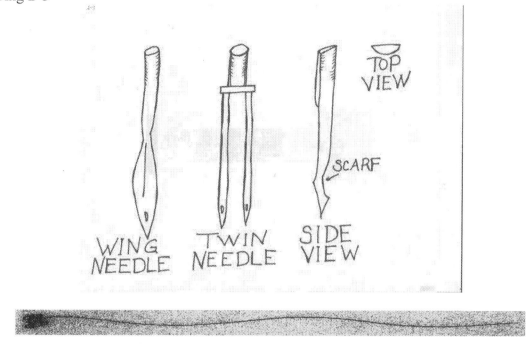

Photo 2-9

Sewing machine stores and the internet will have a wide assortment to choose from.

2-8) Tendency…By the way, when was the last time you changed your sewing machine needle?

The Problem …."Uh huh!" Before we knew any better we used to sew with the same needle until it practically fell out of the machine. NOT GOOD! A needle in bad condition could actually fray the thread and interrupt your sewing progress: even damage the fabric. Still worse, it could impair the *hook* in the bobbin case area, sending you to the sewing machine technician for a hefty *repair bill*. Oh Nooooooo!

To Clarify……..Today we have many different needles that are made for the new fabrics. How marvelous, but, all these choices can be a bit overwhelming. Example: *stretch needles* for *Spandex*; *leather needles* for leather; *wing needles* for heirloom sewing; et cetera. (Drawing 2-8) Singer needles can only be used on Singer Machines. For all other machines, the *Schmetz* brand needle is of better quality and it actually costs less. Therefore, when you have your *Singer* machine serviced, have the technician calibrate it to the Schmetz needle. Using the wrong needle will cause damage to the bobbin area. Note: Rosie at Sew Pros in San Diego County suggested that you remove the needle after you have sewed 8-10 hours or two garments. Do not replace it until you get ready to sew your next project. This way you will not have to guess what type of needle is in the machine: (example, a *ball-point needle* will have much difficulty sewing tightly woven fabrics). Thanks Rosie! Nice save!

2-9) Tendency…"Needles, which one do I use? *Titanium* (Wow! That sounds impressive); *Wing*; *Stretch*; *Universal*; *Twin*; *Quilting*, et cetera. Gee, when I first starting sewing we did not have all these amazingly choices.

The Problem….When sewing woven fabrics, if you are using a Ball Point needle there is a potential for a problem. The needle with the ball point tip can not penetrate some woven fabrics and can force the fabric into the hole of the needle plate below the foot. It happened to one of my students while in class. I had to surgically remove the fabric from the machine. My student was fortunate to be taking my class at Hancock Fabric store. She saved time and gas money because she did not have to drive to the store. She was able to purchase, right then and there, the extra fabric to replace the damaged section and the correct needle. The *Ball Point* needle is designed to slip in-between the yarns of the knit fabrics. Sharp pointed needles can pierce the yarn creating a run in the fabric much like the runs in your panty hose. As Winnie the Pooh would say, "Oh, Bother". Humm! I do not believe Winnie wares panty hose! But, I think you get the idea.

To Clarify……..Here are the basics: *Ball Point* only for knits (sizes 12,14,16, the higher numbers are for heavier fabrics: the lower numbers are for delicate fabrics); the *Universal* has the widest range of sizes 7 – 19, but remember it has a tiny ball point so tightly woven fabrics will not respond well. The most important needle type in my sewing basket and the one I use almost exclusively is the *Jean/Denim* needles sizes 10 – 12 – 14 – 16. The needle has a triangular cut at the point offering an excellent penetration into the layers of fabric. *Titanium* is a fairly new member of the sewing machine needle family and is very strong. Remember the shelf life – one to two garments then toss in the round file. Needle heaven! No exceptions! There are more needles to choose from but I will not be covering them in this book. Check with your sewing teacher or the people working in the sewing machine stores. They have a wealth of knowledge eager to share with you. Also, use the sewing magazines articles and ads as a reference.

Drawing 2-10

-a-   -b-

Photo 2-11

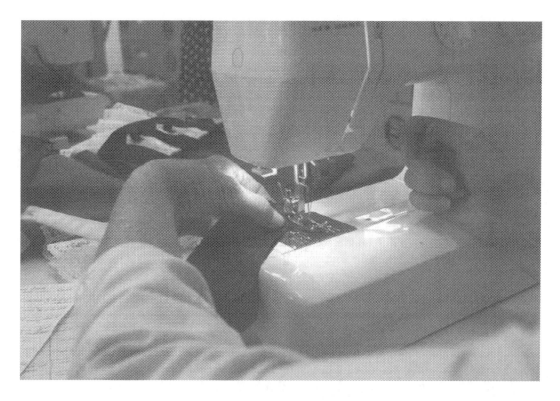

I was in the process of sewing a Captain Hooks costume when this picture was taken.

2-10) Tendency…"Why does my seam have long stitches and short stitches?"

The Problem…….Your machine is skipping stitches: they will not hold. (Drawing 2-10a)

To Clarify……Check your needle. If you suspect it is dull or damaged, it probably is. Any item with a sharp point or cutting surface will eventually become dull or fabricate a burr. To find out if your needle is damaged, lower the foot with a scrap of fabric under it and place you right hand on the hand wheel. As you turn the wheel forward, (like a Waterfall)*, listen carefully. I usually bend down so my ear is near the needle in question. If you hear a crunching sound as the needle penetrates the fabric, **send that needle to needle heaven** (the trash) and install the proper needle. You will find your stitching will immediately improve. Rule of thumb: toss your needle after one or two sewing projects or 8-10 sewing hours. As far as the *serging machine* goes, you must change **both** needles at the same time. There is a really neat little tool you can purchase that makes this task trouble-free. It keeps you from loosing your needle in the bobbin case area (sewing machine) and the looper area (serging machine), the *Needle Inserter*. (Drawing 2-10b) A must buy and make sure to keep it handy. Do not let anyone take it from your machine. My mother, bless her heart, would have to wait for me to come over to insert the needle in her machine. Now she does not have to wait for me. Isn't progress grand?

2-11) Tendency…You have finished sewing the seam and now you are ready to pull the fabric from the machine, but it will not budge.
The Problem ….. New sewers will try to remove the fabric from the machine with the needle still in the fabric. If you really try, you may bend the needle and damage the fabric. This might not effect your sewing now, but that bent needle will give you trouble later. Big time!

To Clarify……*Take a moment*. Ask yourself; is the needle in the down position? Note: Many new machines are computerized today stopping the needle in the up or down position (not in-between) when you stop sewing. Some machines have buttons or icons on screen to program the needle position. This action will raise or lower the needle automatically. Nice feature! There are two ways of raising the needle: 1) push the needle up/down button to raise it; or, 2) for manual sewing machines, turn the hand wheel **forward**, like a Waterfall*, until the *take up lever* is at its highest point. In class I put my hand in front of the needle as my students turn the hand wheel. This way she/he can not look at the needle. Just because the needle is up does not mean the take-up lever is all the way up.) Now you can lift the foot and remove the fabric from the machine. Tip: hold the fabric as close to the end of the seam as possible and gently but firmly pull it out towards the <u>back left corner</u>. (Photo 2-11) The benefit: this will help you keep the fabric from gathering up at the end of the seam line. {In the photo my wrist is bent quite a bit because I had to lower my shoulder to get it out of the cameras' view making this shot very uncomfortable for me. Oh what we put ourselves through to get that perfect shot.}

*See *take-up-lever* in Section III Tendency 7-1, page 56.

Drawing 2-12

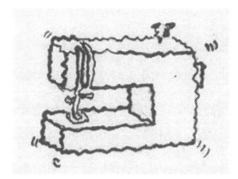

2-12) Tendency...NEEDLE BROKEN

The Problem......For those of you who have a computerized sewing machine, **this is scary**. The machine shakes violently and makes a terrible sound. (Drawing 2-12) One cause is when you start sewing without checking to see what foot you have in the machine. Unfortunately this could damage the foot and **will** break the needle. Example: If you have been using a zipper foot, and you change the stitch to a zigzag and/or move the needle position, the needle will slam down on the foot causing the turmoil and a shock to your nerves system. Also, you will get the same results if you are preparing to sew a zig-zag stitch using the *straight stitch throat plate*. The plate has a small hole and is used primarily for delicate fabric: definitely a valuable tool. The throat plate can be installed using screws or sliding it into place. Check your manual for details and when in doubt ask your sewing teacher, or a reputable sewing machine dealer.

To Clarify.........**Get your machine turned off fast**. Remember, it only takes a moment to make sure you have the correct foot and or throat plate for the sewing job you are about to commence. Not to mention saving your needle from needle heaven before its time. Hint: After you finish sewing with your specialty feet (blind hem, straight stitch, button foot, et cetera) remove it and leave the ankle naked. Ooh!

Notions~~~~Notions~~~~and~~~~even~~~~more~~~~Notions

This is just a small section of the notions wall.
On one of the very bottom pegs is a little known and rather
difficult item to find, the *collar tabs* for your husbands shirt collar.

3 Just a Few Sewing Notions Worth Noting

Drawing 3-1

-a-

-b-

-c-

Drawing 3-2

3-1) Tendency…"String! Thread! What is the difference?" (Drawing 3-1a)

The Problem……We all know what string is used for: tie up packages; hang small pictures; hold together a bundle of kindling plus other stuff. But string is not satisfactory for sewing. Besides it is to fat to put through the eye of most needles.

To Clarify………Quality sewing threads are made-up of long staples with a high degree of twist. Regular sewing thread is *3 ply*. The <u>3 long stapled yarns</u> are twisted together making the thread smooth and strong: the preferred thread for your sewing machine. 100% Polyester thread is strong and slightly stretchy. {"..it slips through the fabric easily and the stitches "bed down" to create inconspicuous seams."*} Heirloom sewing and quilts are usually made from 100% cotton. It is best to use 100% cotton thread, also 3 ply. The serger thread is *2 ply*. It is too weak to use in the regular sewing machine. But it is on target for *serging machines*. Cheap thread is made-up of short staples with slubs (fuss balls) throughout making it weak. When buying thread, stay away from the 10 for $5 bargains. Not good. They will cause many problems, such as: thread breakage, thread jams, kinking up, et cetera. Case-in-point: During class I explain the good and the bad of threads. Student A uses the bad thread. Incase you are wondering, old thread is no better. The other students use Gutermann and Mettler brands. After a while student "A" starts having problems with her seams as well as her machine while the rest of the class progresses without a hitch. I smile as my students realized what works and what does not. Speaking of Gutermann and Mettler thread – notice how the thread is wound on the spools. The thread is wound in a cress cross fashion making it whip off the spool as you sew. The horizontal spool pin probably works best with these spools. Some times I use a separate unit (Drawing 3-1c) placed at the back of the machine. It consists of a platform with two vertical posts. The center post is for the thread spool. The outer post – much longer with a hook on top – pulls and guides the thread from the spool up through the hook then to the sewing machine. The most common spool pin is the vertical post(s). Be sure you have the *felt cushion* under the spool; it helps the spool turn smoothly while operating the sewing machine. Look at the ads in the *Threads Magazine* for the different threads available to sewers. Drawing 3-1b shows several special threads, there are many more threads available in stores and on-line. Have fun with them.

3-2) Tendency…Thread's cheap, right? 5 for $1? Wow!

To Clarify…….Don't go there. (Drawing 3-2) I am going to repeat myself because it bears repeating. Thread is made-up of three "yarns". Each yarn is made-up of <u>long staples</u>. Cheap thread is made up of short stables. This will cause plenty of trouble with your stitches. The thread breaks often and those little fuss balls get caught in the tension discs and other places. Cleaning often is a necessity. I see students pulling a long thread tail off the spool and wrapping the thread round and round their hand in preparation to thread the machine. This usually is a waist of thread. Besides, the thread will get caught on just about anything in its path. In the end you will just have to cut the excess off and toss it in the trash. What ever you do don't drop too many threads on the carpet, they will get caught in the vacuum roller brush and could cause the belt to melt down. Nasty smell! It is a good idea to take the roller brush off and clean it often.

To Clarify………While threading your machine, just pull off enough thread to make a 3"to 4" thread tail. As you reel the thread from the spool, it will give you enough thread to place it through the thread guides. For *serger thread*, the problem is even more pronounced because the weight of the thread is so light, only two ply, and there are many more areas it could get hung-up on. As Winnie the Pooh would say, "Oh, Bother".*See Articles and Quotes, page iv.

Drawing 3-3

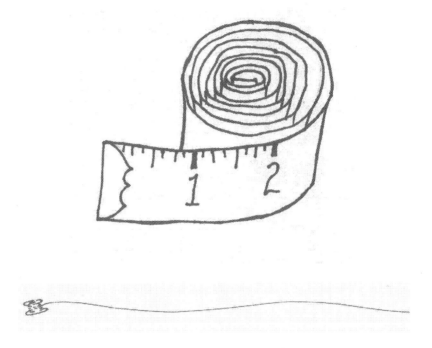

Photo 3-4

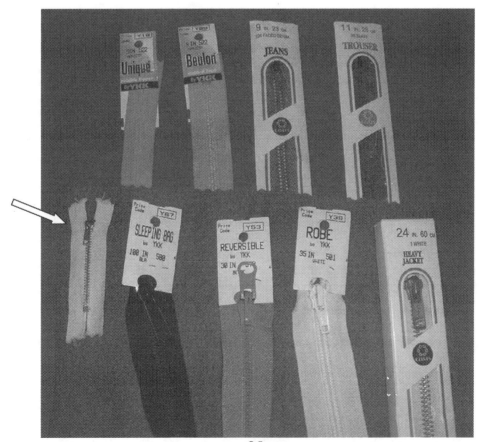

3-3) Tendency…You were in such a hurry today you just dumped your tools and notions in the sewing basket including the very long and vulnerable *measuring tape.*

The Problem….The measuring tape will develop creases and will make it difficult to use. And the tape can get tangled up in all sorts of things in your sewing basket: including thread. It can get mighty unpleasant while trying to untangle the measuring tape from the thread. Have you ever accidentally <u>cut</u> your measuring tape? Things happen when you are in a hurry!

To Clarify………I encourage my students to take just a *very few moments* to roll up their 60 inch measuring tape. (Drawing 3-3) Go ahead, start rolling. A few words on the 120 inch tape: it is too clumsy for garment projects. However the longer tape is excellent for quilting projects. As you read this, pick it up and coil the tape at the 60 inch or 120 inch end. This way the one inch end is not crimped. Now the measuring tape will nestle nicely inside the sewing basket and not get tangled up in other stuff. By the time you have read this passage your tape would be coiled and ready to store properly. Yes! Now, this does not mean we always have time to do it right now. So the next time you open your sewing basket, coil up your measuring tape immediately.

3-4) Tendency…It is too easy to purchase the wrong zipper: wrong size; wrong color; wrong style! Too many wrongs do not make a right!

The Problem….“Oh, Bother” said Pooh. Now you have to go back to the store and it is probably 11PM and the fabric stores are closed.

To Clarify……..As a former *Hancock Fabric Store* cashier, I would ask my customers what they were purchasing the zipper for. More often than not we would walk over to the zipper display to fetch the right one. You have your *metal teeth* and your *plastic coils.* Then you have your *rhinestone zipper teeth.* They are so cool! Did you know you can buy a *100 inch zipper*? A sleeping bag needs a very long zipper and this one fits the bill nicely. A friend loaned her *Barbie Doll two inch zipper* for this photo, see arrow. (Photo 3-4) Thanks Candace! There are *light weight zippers* and *separating zippers.* Some separate at one end only and then others have pull tabs inside and outside. Wow! The confusion is enough to grab your sewing teacher for help. One zipper I used to use often was the *dress placate zipper.* It has been many years since I have seen this one in the stores. It was closed at both ends so you could sew it into the side seam under the sleeve. Styles change and so did zippers. The other day I was rummaging through my stash of notions and came up with several dress placate zippers. I discovered an excellent use for the placate zippers for today’s fashions: the purse closures. Works Great! Now I have more room in my notions storage for more stash!

Photo 3-5

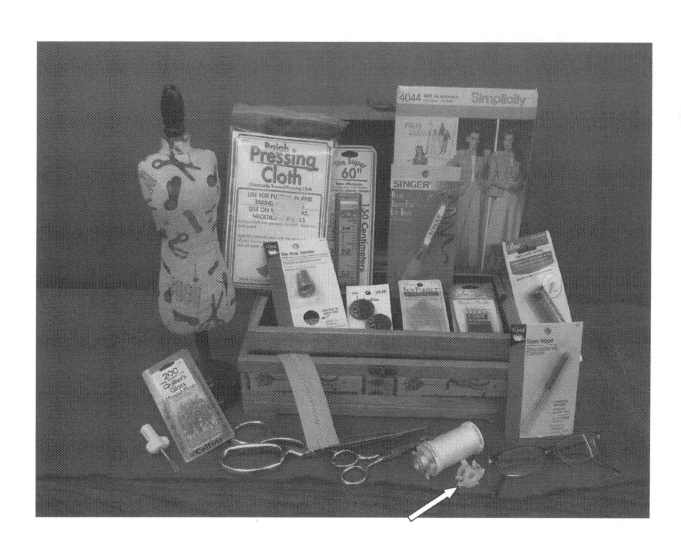

3-5) Tendency…"What are notions? What is the bare minimum needed to start sewing?"

The Problem….Sewing in general is confusing. I see beginners agonizing over what notions they need. Some buy the convenient packaged notions. The convenient packaged starter sets are really bad: hardly anyone uses the tracing wheel; the shears are the worst; the seam ripper is awful and the measuring tape is hard to read. Well, so much for convenience.

To Clarify………You do not need all kinds of gadgets especially those you probable will not use for some time, if ever. Established seamstresses, professional tailors and sewing teachers (including myself) posse many tools. But when we started we only had a few 'toys', such as:

60" tape measure (the kind that does not stretch)

6" seam gauge, an absolute must [I goofed and didn't get it in the picture!]

A pair of *bent handled fabric shears* that <u>feels good</u> in your hand and at least 8"

Pin cushion – I have the traditional tomato plus a 9" dress form and an overstuffed chair, fun

Glass head long silk pins, my favorite

Thread cutting scissors with a sharp point or *thread snips* plus *paper scissors*

Seam ripper (my Australian students call it a seam picker) buy the one with a glass ball

Several *Handi Bobs* (see arrow)

Short screw driver with "ears"

Hand sewing needles – *Sharps* variety package

Jeans needles one package of each *sizes 10-12-14*

Marking chalk, Clover has a good one

Several *bandages*

*S*ewing basket, I also have a small *cosmetic bag* works well for traveling to class

These are the essentials to get you started. Do use reading glasses if you need them. More sewing toys will come as your needs dictate. Ex: an Aul, a point turner, seams great, et cetera. (Handi Bobs fit on the thread spool and house the bobbin that has the same thread wound on it. These are fantastic. See arrow. They help keep my sewing basket tidy. And a neat basket is a productive basket. Just thought you would like to know.)

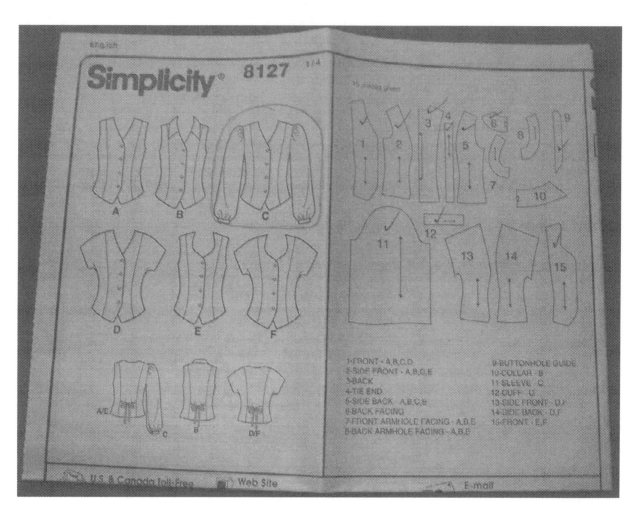

Circle the view you want to make and check the pattern pieces you will need.

4 The Different Parts of the Pattern

4-1   Cutting out the fabric on the fold line of the pattern

4-2   Trying to pin a wrinkled pattern

4-3   What is interfacing? What is facing? Why do I need it?

4-4   Darts? What are they?

4-5   Some design features are too difficult for beginners

4-6   There are all kinds of printed marks on the pattern

Drawing 4-1

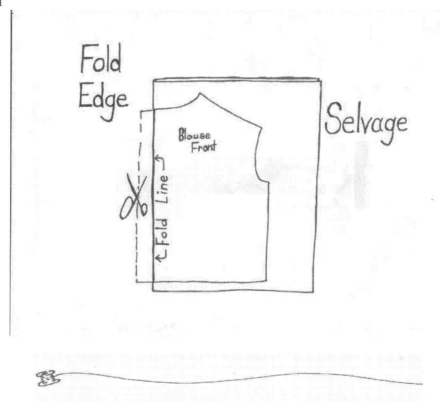

Fold
Edge

Selvage

Blouse
Front

Fold Line

Photo 4-2

From this fabric, I made a Hawaiian Western shirt to ware to the Costume College!
Lovely Hula Hands and Yippi-Kayah-Yay!

4-1) Tendency…"Help! I just cut out the fabric where it should have been on the fold line."

The Problem…..Beginners cut off the excess paper surrounding the *paper pattern pieces* all the way around and are unaware that not all edges are cutting lines. Not realizing they should place the pattern piece on the fold line, beginners place the piece inside the fabric away from the fold and cut all the way around the pattern. A loose fitting garment is not to bad, but a snug fitting garment, well, "Houston, we have a problem!" In class we develop rather inventive solutions. Necessity being the mother of invention certainly applies here.

To Clarify……Most pattern pieces state on the paper to: Cut 2; or, Cut 1 on the fold line. The fold line tells us the pattern represents ½ of the piece. Example: the front dress section usually has no center seam. So, I recommend not cutting the *tissue paper pattern* on the fold line. Instead, cut around it by leaving a strip of the paper next to the fold line. (Drawing 4-1) When you get ready to pin the pattern to the fabric, this will scream at you to **place this pattern piece on the fold of the fabric!** Nice save! As for a loose fitting garment, making as narrow a SA (seam allowance) is one way to save the day. If this is not an option, "listen" to the fabric, it may reveal the solution. I hope I have made my self perfectly clear on this costly subject.

4-2) Tendency…Trying to pin a wrinkled pattern.

The Problem….You will not get an accurate cut if the pattern pieces have deep creased. (Photo 4-2) Besides, crushing the paper pattern weakens the paper and it could tear easily.

To Clarify……..As to the question, "What did you learn in sewing class today?" your answer could be: "I learned to #1 press paper and #2 iron threads." The person asking will be either impressed or confused. #1 I recommend pressing the pattern on the underside of the paper, printed words facing down. Pressing the pattern with words up will cause the tissue paper to curl up making it difficult to pin. Set the iron temperature gauge control at the start of the steam dial, this will do just fine. Start at the center of the pattern. Holding the paper down with your free hand, move the iron to the outer edge of the pattern. Make sure the iron is flat to the board and NO STEAM. Do this quickly; you don't want to scorch the paper. Repeat until the paper is reasonably smooth. There may be faint creases but this will not hamper your cutting task. #2 As to ironing the thread trick: after running the thread through a special *thread wax* (can be found in fabric stores or the internet) place the thread under the iron and pull the thread making sure it slides all the way under the iron: pressing down as you go. This will straighten the thread keeping it from getting tangled and knotted while hand sewing. And this technique will allow you an easier time threading your needle: another measurable benefit.

Drawing 4-3

Photo 4-3

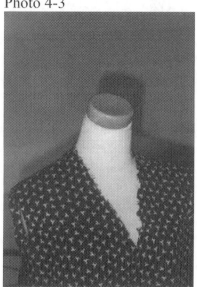

Fabric
Key

RIGHT SIDE | WRONG SIDE | # INTER- FACING # | LINING

Drawing 4-4

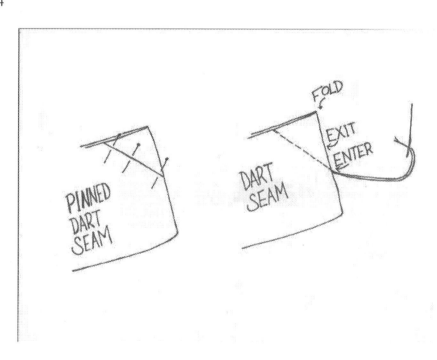

PINNED DART SEAM

DART SEAM

FOLD

EXIT
ENTER

4-3) Tendency…What is facing? What is interfacing? Why do I need them?

The Problem.......In the first place, beginning sewers do not understand why they need to purchase additional fabric for interfacing, Secondly, facing pattern pieces are a mystery. After all you do not see it, do you?

To Clarify........The *facings* are usually cut from the fashion fabric. Your pattern will have pieces that state: Facing – cut 2 or Cut 1 on fold. On-the-other-hand, some facings are merely the fashion fabric turned twice towards the inside: generally, each turn measures ¼ to ½ inch deep. This does a couple of things: finishes the cut or raw edges and gives the neck or armhole added strength so it will not stretch out of shape. At the writing of this book it was popular to have unfinished edges. (Photo 4-3) *Interfacing* by its name means another fabric is placed between the garment fabric and the facing or lining. The truth bee known, interfacing helps shape a garment in special areas such as: waistbands; neck openings; buttonholes and buttons; plus a host of other areas in a tailored garment. If there is no interfacing the garment will not hold its shape and droop in the most dreadful places. Reading the pattern instruction page either 1 or 2, the interfacing is indicated by the # sign. (Drawing 4-3) The finished product will stretch out of shape if you do not include interfacing in your garment sewing. Buttonholes will fall apart and the fabric where the button is sewed will tare apart and the button will dangle from your shirt. Yuck! See, you really need the special fabric known as interfacing. I prefer the sew in interfacing for garments, but iron-on works well when sewing handbags and home décor projects. Quilters like the batting that has the iron-on capability.

4-4) Tendency….Darts? What are they? Where do you use them?

The Problem ....The hardest part of sewing a dart is at the tip. To do this we must sew the dart seams <u>absolutely</u> straight. Beginners tend to curve inward or outward as they reach the tip of the dart where the fold is. This will look rather odd on your body.

To Clarify........A dart helps you take a one dimensional fabric and sculpt it into a three dimensional garment to fit the curves of your body. Before you take the pattern off the fabric, mark the dart placement. I use Tailors Tacks (See Drawing 13-1, pages 101) then carefully remove the pattern. Next, fold the fabric to make the dart by lining up the Tailors Tacks and pin exactly on each Tailors Tack through both layers of fabric. Next take a ruler and draw a straight line (use *Tailors chalk*) from the cut edge to the tip of the dart. Always start sewing the dart at the widest point and sew towards the end of the marked line at the folded edge. Slow down and make one stitch off the fabric: <u>with the hand wheel</u>. Remove the fabric and cut a three inch thread tail. (Drawing 4-4) This next step I call the "<u>Legend of the Disappearing Thread</u>." Using a hand needle, thread the tail ends into the eye of the needle. Slip the needle in exactly where you stopped sewing with the machine. Slide it as far as you can along the fold. Exit the fabric and cut the thread tails. Like magic, the threads disappear, but the seam stays intact. I have always been uncomfortable with back stitching in the small area at the dart tip. The feed dogs can not hold the fabric while you sew in reverse causing the stitches to pucker the fabric. This could cause a thread lock. "Oh Bother", said Winnie the Pooh. Not much good when you attempt to a reverse stitch to anchor the threads at the dart point. The same goes for tying the thread tails at the point. I have had the knot come loose. unfortunately the dart starts to come undone. Note: A sign of a well made garment is when there are not traces of thread tails.

Photo 4-5

Drawing 4-6

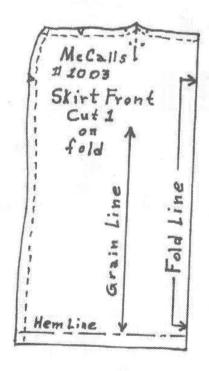

McCalls
#1003
Skirt Front
Cut 1
on
fold

Grain Line

Fold Line

Hem Line

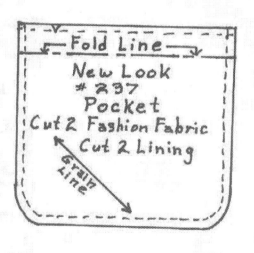

Fold Line

New Look
#237
Pocket
Cut 2 Fashion Fabric
Cut 2 Lining

Grain
Line

4-5) Tendency…Sewing spaghetti straps, sleeves, fly front zippers, and collars (Photo 4-5 see arrow), are not for beginners.

The Problem….These design features are frustrating until you know how to read the pattern instructions. Example: lay zipper face down on the right front section…., I'm already confused.

To Clarify….…Sewing is not easy. It takes time, practice, and a sewing teacher to help you develop the following skills: your hands; ability to read and understand the instruction pages; as well as a good understanding of your sewing machine. Don't forget the makings on the pattern pieces. My advice is to start with a shell top or the popular (in 2003-4) flannel pajama bottoms (commonly known as PJ's). Even these can be confusing when sewing the right and left legs together at the crouch seam producing a funny looking pant. Ripping out and starting over is the next task: that is if you plan to wear them. Ask your sewing teacher for help to avoid the time wasted ripping out. In my tiny sewing class room at the *JoAnn Fabric Store,* I had nine Girl Scouts sewing PJ's. We came up with all sorts of interesting leg combinations. We had fun!

4-6) Tendency…"There are all kinds of printed marks on the pattern, I'm hopelessly lost"

The Problem….When you do not understand how to read the pattern pieces you will probably cut on the fold line or not pin the pattern piece to the appropriate fabric or worse, ignore the Grain line.

To Clarify….…Get to a sewing class! If you have time before class, read page one of the instruction sheet. Included are detailed instructions for each marking. Now look at the pattern pieces. First locate the name of the pattern company, (Drawing 4-6) the pattern number and what the piece represents, example: skirt front. Next see how many layers of fabric you will be cutting. Note the *Grain Line* or the *Fold Line*. There are several diamonds or triangles along the cutting lines. When I first learned to sew I was encouraged to cut OUT the triangle shapes along this cutting line. This was very awkward, painful and all too often not accurate. When it came to sewing the front piece to the back piece the points did not match causing the hem to have one section longer then the other. Today I cut straight across where the triangles are printed. Before removing the pattern I use the tip of my good *sharp shears* to cut a slit <u>within</u> the 5/8 inch SA. It is important to only cut half way to the sewing line. Sewing with a serger will be OK as long as you plan to use the blade to cut off the excess SA. Otherwise cut out the triangle because a slit into the fabric will ravel leaving a hole, oops! Or, better yet: use a *hand needle* and thread to sew a running stitch for about 3 inches starting at the tip of the diamond in each fabric piece. This takes time but it will increase the likelihood of a successfully finished project.

Fabric Conversion Chart

Fabric Width	35"/36"	38"/39"	44"/45"	48"/50"	54"/56"	58"/60"
Y	1-3/4	1-1/2	1-3/8	1-1/4	1-1/8	1
A	2	1-3/4	1-5/8	1-1/2	1 3/8	1-1/4
R	**2-1/4**	2	1-3/4	1-5/8	1-1/2	1-3/8
D	2-1/2	2-1/4	1/8	1-3/4	1-3/4	1-5/8
A	2-7/8	2-1/2	2-1/4	2	1-7/8	1-3/4
G	3-1/8	2-3/4	2-1/2	2-1/4	2	1-7/8
E	3-3/8	3	2-3/4	2-3/8	2-1/4	2
*	3-3/4	3-1/4	2-7/8	2-5/8	2-3/8	2-1/4
*	4-1/4	3-1/2	3-1/8	2-3/4	2-5/8	2-3/8
*	4-1/2	3-3/4	3-3/8	3	2-3/4	2-5/8
*	4-3/4	4	3-5/8	3-1/4	2-7/8	2-3/4
*	5	4-1/4	3-7/8	3-3/8	3-1/8	2-7/8

If your pattern calls for 1-3/4 yards of 44"/45" wide fabric and you are purchasing 35"/36" wide fabric, run your finger down the 44"/45" column and across to the 35"/36" column. You will need 2-1/4 yards of the 35"/36" wide fabric. See, it is simple when you crack the code!

#5 Fabric Talk

5-1   After I washed my garment it shrank. What happened?

5-2   Certain fabrics can be difficult to sew for beginners

5-3   Trying to pin wrinkled or creased fabric

5-4   What is the selvage edge?   What do you mean folded edge?

5-5   Salvage or Selvage, which is it?

5-6   What do I do with all these scraps?

Drawing 5-1

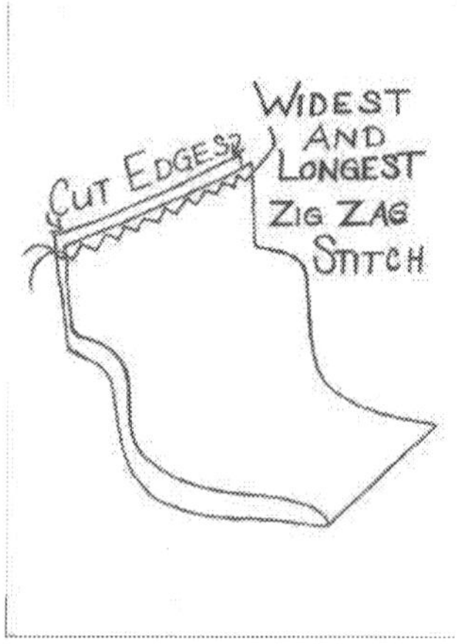

-a-

WIDEST AND LONGEST ZIG ZAG STITCH

CUT EDGES?

-b-

Photo 5-2

U.S. $20.00 CAN. $27.50 ⬤ GREEN AVERAGE,

7539

MISSES'/MISSES' PETITE COAT Very loose-fit-ting, flared, lined coat, below mid-knee, has collar, slightly extended shoulders, shoulder pads, side pockets and long, two-piece sleeves. A: button vent, and lining forms trim effect. B: button trim and optional purchased trim.

NOTIONS: Coat A,B: ½" (13mm) Shoulder Pads or Vogue # 9723, Four ⅞" (22mm) Buttons, Six ¾" (20mm) Buttons and (Opt.) ¼" (6mm) Twill Tape. Also for B: (Opt.) ⅛" (3mm) Piping: 4¼ yds. (3.9m) for Sizes 8 to 12, 4½ yds. (4.2m) for Sizes 14 to 18 and 4⅞ yds. (4.5m) for Sizes 20 to 24.

FABRICS: Novelty Wools, Silk-like Tweeds and Flannel. Lining: Shantung and Crepe de Chine. Interfacing A,B: Sew-In Hair Canvas. Suitable for everything except obvious diagonals. Even/uneven plaids/stripes will not match at side seams. *with nap. **without nap.

MANTEAU L
au-dessous
doublé, av
épaulettes
poches du
nées et dou
ture de bo
MERCERIE
ou faites e
4 (22mm),
(6mm); pi
(3mm): 3.9
18); 4.5m (
TISSUS: La
- Flanelle
Chine. Ent
place. Gre
Rayures/b
ennent. Ra
aux coutur

SIZE	(8	10	12)	(14	16	18)	(20	22	24)	TAILLE (8
Fabric widths given in inches.										Largeurs d
COAT A										MANTEAU
45"	3⅝	3¾	3¾	3⅞	3⅞	4	4	4¼	4¼	115" 3.5
60"										

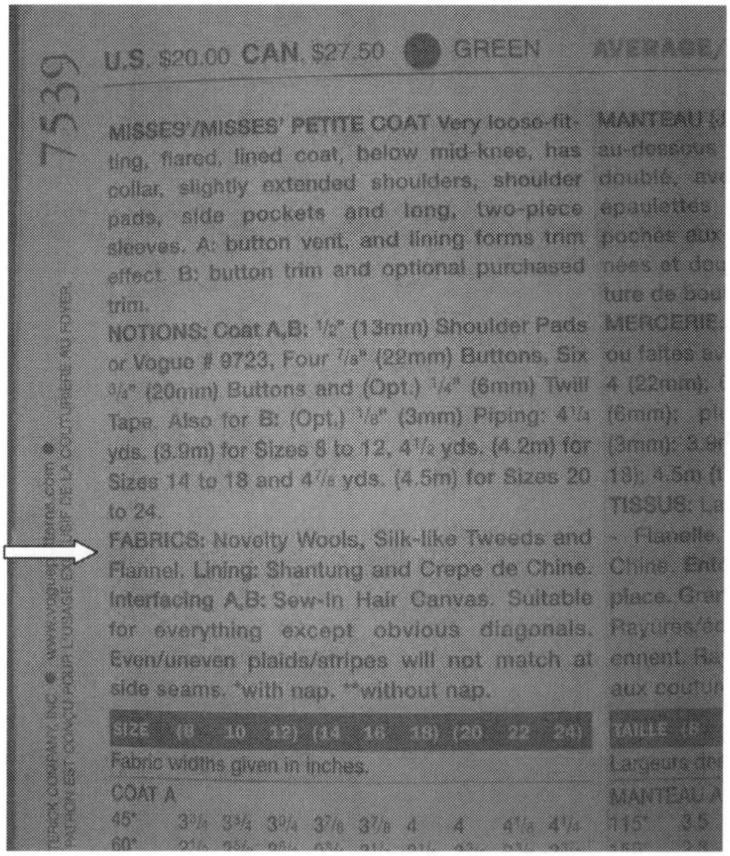

5-1) Tendency…"After I washed my garment it shrank. What happened?"

The Problem….We are always in a hurry to start our next sewing project. However, not *washing or dry cleaning* all the fabrics & trims will probably guarantee the finished project will shrink. (Drawing 5-1a) Especially when sewing with cotton. And then there is the sizing. The manufacturers dip or spray sizing onto the fabric to assure a quality produce while in transit to your favorite fabric store. The sizing makes some fabrics stiff and difficult to sew. Zippers do not need to be preshrunk, but all trims do.

To Clarify……..First you need to determine how you will clean your finished garments and home decorative projects. Printed on the end of the bolt you will find either a cleaning code or cleaning instructions. When in doubt ask the lady at your fabric store. When dry cleaning, ask to have your fabric *steam-pressed flat, not folded.* (Dry cleaning fabrics and finished garments look better and last longer, however, bee aware of the cost.) I use sew-in woven interfacing and preshrink it along with the fashion fabrics. I recommend placing all cut edges of each fabric together, NOT THE SELVAGE (finished) EDGES. (See Drawing 5-4 pages 41 – 42) Next, sew the <u>widest and longest PLAIN zig zag stitch</u> using your sewing machine. (Drawing 5-1b) You need to sew this right at the cut edge of your fabric. This minimizes the fabric from fraying as it goes through the washer/dryer or dry cleaning process. Use a thread you will be able to see, example: pink thread on black fabric. After cleaning simply rip the stitches out, the wide-long zigzag stitch will come out fairly easily. After washing press the fabric with a press cloth or a protected iron. For washed pieces, it is best to press the fabric flat on the wrong side before you cut. An excellent practice is to cut the front bodice for a wedding gown from fabric rolled flat on a tube instead of fabric folded on a bolt. This eliminates that ugly crease that never seems to steam out. A word of causation: the folded edge is not always on the straight of the grain (parallel to the selvage edge) and could make the finished garment hang curiously funny. Personally I do not know anyone who wants to ware strangely weird looking clothes. Note: because knits generally do not ravel, this sewing step is not necessary. *Threads Magazine* #118 page 38 has a fabulous article to read: "Wash your stash", by Judith Newkam. Not only sound advice, but interesting possibilities abound.

5-2) Tendency…Certain fabrics can be difficult to sew for beginners even some experienced sewers. Fabrics like: corduroy; Peachskin; fake fur; satin, and velvet. (Photo 5-2)

The Problem….The huge variety of fabrics produced today are absolutely fascinating and discouraging all at the same time. There is the weave and the fiber content and the texture and the direction of the print and the weight and the drape and I think you are getting the idea that there are many factors to contend with. Halloween costume sewing is an excellent example: exciting, fun and bewildering. The whole process of choosing fabrics can be mind boggling.

To Clarify……..The best fabrics to start with are 100% wool -very forgiving and malleable- and 100% cotton -a nice variety of weights. My first timers want to sew with fabrics like: satins, velvets, stretch woven, and Rayon. Eeeegads! What's a body to do? These and many currently popular fabrics can discourage the beginner. My advise is to make a few sewing projects out of the 100% stuff first. Most combinations of Poly/Cotton are sewing friendly. These fabrics will offer you a chance to develop your new sewing skills and not tear your hair out in frustration.

Photo 5-3

Creased on purpose! but could be difficult to sew.

Drawing 5-4

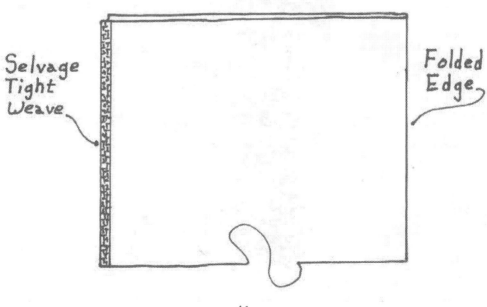

Selvage
Tight
Weave

Folded
Edge

5-3) Tendency...Trying to pin wrinkled or creased fabric.

The Problem....Generally when you cut pattern piece out of your fashion fabric, you cut two fabric layers at a time. If there are creases or wrinkles, the two pieces will not be the same. This causes problems when trying to match the appropriate piece to its counter piece. The fabric in Photo 5-3 is creased on purpose. I do not recommend this fabric for beginners. If you are more experienced, give this type of fabric a try, but do not iron out or steam these creases, after all you probably paid a handsome price for those creases.

To Clarify........To prepare the wrinkled fabric use steam sparingly until you know how the fabric responds. Open out the fabric (single layer) and press it smooth <u>on the wrong side</u>. Pay particular attention on the creased center fold line. Very often this center fold is not on the straight of the grain. By pressing out the crease, lining up the selvage edges will be more successful. Continue pressing on the wrong side of the fabric. (I am a former teacher for the <u>Kids Can Sew Program</u>, by Carolyn Curtis. She called the wrong side of the fabric, "Ugly side" and the right side, "Pretty side", the kids, their parents and I loved her clever drawings and text.) Using a *press cloth* is a must when pressing wool, silk, Rayon, polyester, and some blended fabrics. You do not want to get a shine on the surface of the fabric. Man-made fabrics like polyester require a cooler iron to avoid melting the fibers. Some fabrics do not require much pressing because the weave or texture is more or less permanent such as *seersucker*. Smashing! So many fabrics: so many techniques. Keep sewing, you will get the hang of it! When working with pile fabrics, such as velvet, it is a good idea to use a special pressing tool called, *Needle Board*. Special Note: Photo on page 93 shows my *Elna Press*. I really like to use this press when my fabric is wrinkled. The *Press* costs a bit but if you decide you like sewing, this is a good investment. Another benefit: I get a really great crease on my slacks. [Note: It is <u>not</u> a good idea to press open the seam allowance on fleece fabric, but then, sewing fleece is much better on the serging machine making pressing unnecessary. Serging a fleece project is quick, too. Nice time saver.]

5-4) Tendency...What is the selvage edge?   What do you mean folded edge?

The Problem....It is a simple matter of learning the language.

To Clarify........Woven fabric starts with lengthwise (*Warp*) yarns attached to a loom. The filling or crosswise yarns (*Weft*) are moved by a shuttle horizontally back and forth through the *Warp* yarns. The outer two edges are called the selvage edge. The weave is tighter at the edges than the interior of the finished fabric. After the fabric is woven some fabrics are folded in half lengthwise (selvage edges together) and placed on a bolt, creating the *folded edge*. (Drawing 5-4) Upholstery and drapery fabrics generally are rolled on to a tube. When sewing home décor projects you can use the selvage edge provided you cut slits, at an angle, into the selvage at regular intervals. This relieves the tightness. For garment sewing using the selvage is not advisable. The selvage edge will pucker in your seam no mater how many times you slit the selvage. Not Good!

Drawing 5-5

Photo 5-6

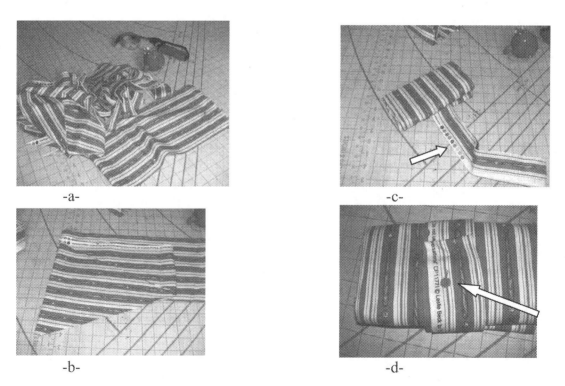

-a-

-b-

-c-

-d-

5-5) Tendency…..I would like to clear up a commonly miss pronounced word. Is it Salvage or Selvage?

The Problem…The only difference between the two words is one little letter: but their meanings are a world apart. Titanic Shipwrecks and Sunken Treasures, page 93 Glossary quote, "Rescue of a wrecked or damaged ship and its cargo". This does not sound like sewing to me!

To Clarify……..Now that you are clear on how to pronounce the words you can feel confident and come across as knowledgeable about sewing stuff as you shop in the fabric store. Take a stroll through the store and feel the different selvage edges of fashion, drapery and upholstery, even knit fabrics. Some selvages are narrow, some are wide. Some drapery and quilting fabrics will weave a color code in the *selvage* area and print the manufacturers name and design of the fabric. (See arrow Photo 5-6 c) Some knit fabric manufacturers slather glue on the selvages. Be sure to cut off this edge, it would not be very comfortable to wear. Just thought you would like to know. Hopefully you can take the time to have fun observing the different selvage edges. For my granddaughters 4th birthday I made a dress out of a border print fabric sewing a strip of the printed salvage, with the name of the design, on the inside of the hem.

(5-6) Tendency…After the pattern is cut out of the fabric there could be large and small useable scraps left over. Some students merely toss the left over scraps away or cram them in a drawer or box.

The Problem……This can be very untidy and a waist of fabric.

To Clarify………After my students finish their cutting, I set the stage for a presentation. First I take the large scraps and layer them on the table, see Photo 5-6a. Then I add the smaller pieces, reserving a long strip of fabric. Next I fold the odd shaped scraps in on the sides and continue to fold, see Photo 5-6b. Do not roll: simply establish a square or rectangle package. Because there will be small packages and really big packages and every size in-between, I find the flat packages stack better then rolled up ones. But that does not mean you couldn't roll them up: this might make an attractive display. Next I tuck the long fairly narrow strip inside the folds, see Photo 5-6c, and firm but gently wrap the strip around and around. You don't want to wrinkle the fabric just keep it contained. Lastly, I take a *long pin* making a stitch (See Tendency 2-4, page 10) through the strip and at least one layer of the fabric package, see Photo 5-6d arrow. Be sure to berry the sharp tip into the fabric. This way you won't stick your self when handling the packages. Now here comes the ceremony: with both hands, I present the neat package to my student. I always get a smile and a thank you. Should you opt to toss the scraps, remember, quilters will jump back flips for these scraps so do not toss them out. Some times I will forgot to cut out all the pattern pieces (pocket or waistband).What an easy task it is to find the fabric package and complete my cutting in a timely manner.

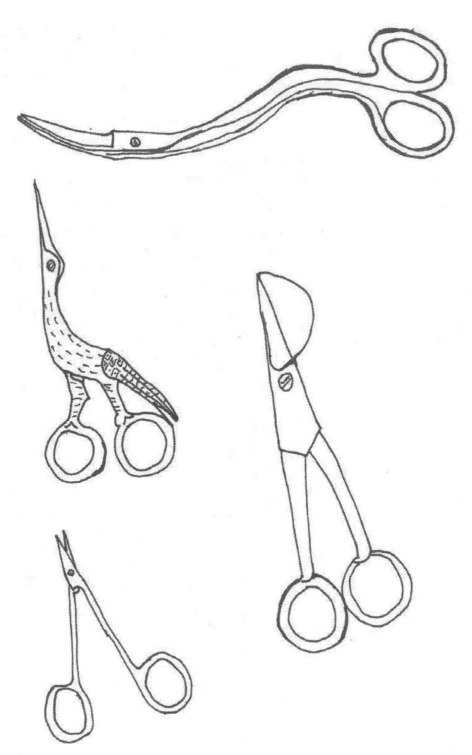

These are just a few special task scissors available to the home sewer! From top clockwise:
Double Bent Embroidery, Duck Bill, Thread and Embroidery Scissors.
Any one using my scissors without permission will experience a painful existence. Ha!

#6   Do **Not** Touch My Fabric Shears

Photo 6-1

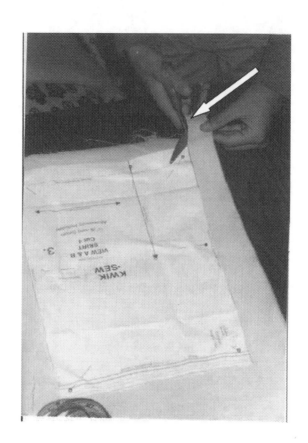

Drawing 6-2

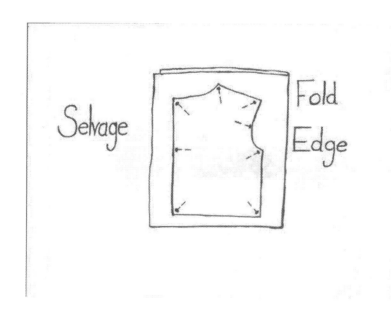

6-1) Tendency…...Tilting scissors while cutting your pattern and fabric.

The Problem……A bad cut will compromise your sewing project. You cannot cut accurately when tilting the *scissors* beyond 90 degrees to the table. (Photo 6-1) You will come up with a beveled cut. Good for picture frames: not for sewing.

To Clarify………The following techniques will help you cut with confidence. 1) Keep the *scissors* absolutely perpendicular to the table as you <u>glide</u> the tip of the scissors along the table. The table will steady your cutting hand. 2) Do not pick-up the scissors while you are cutting in a curve. The benefit: cutting a smoother line. 3) Notice my student is cutting with the pattern to the back of her cutting hand. (See arrow) This way she can peel away the excess fabric with the other hand as she cuts.4) Do not completely close the scissors. Slide scissors open while simultaneously moving forward towards the place where you last cut. Practice this and it will become second nature to you. 5) To avoid damaging your fine table surface, use an *accordion cardboard cutting board*. I have placed the cutting board on the bed, the dining table, even the kitchen counter. A really useful tool! 6) Do not use *pinking shears* to cut out your pattern. They can not cut accurately. In the past we used pinking shears to keep fabric from fraying. For most fabrics it is really better to pink only a single layer at a time. For light weight fabric cutting two layers is better. Today we have the *serging (overcastting)* stitch selection on our sewing machines and of course the *serging machine* itself. What a time saver! Personally, I am grateful for my serging machine: the pinking shears in the past always hurt my thumb. Actually, engineers have finally taken the pain out of *pinking shears* with the advent of the spring mechanism, (see page 51), try it you'll like it! I did!

6-2) Tendency…Incorrect pinning can cause you to cut jagged edges.

The Problem….One would think that pinning parallel to the cutting line would grip the pattern to the fabric allowing you to cut a smooth line. Well…it does, but this only holds a very tiny area. Actually what happens is the fabric and pattern bunch up creating the potential for you to cut an imprecise edge. There are a couple of exceptions: velvet and satin.

To Clarify…….You will secure the pattern to the fabric in a much greater area when you pin about ¾" in from the pattern cutting line and perpendicular to this cut line. Corners pinned at a 45 degree angle will also help you cut the line without distortion. (Drawing 6-2) This one will take some practice. After you have gained confidence in pinning, as described in Tendency 2-3, page 10, you will find this technique really helpful when cutting out your patterns. As for velvet and satin, pinning parallel to the cut edge within the SA avoids pin marks on velvet and permanent holes in satin. What we do to be beautiful boggles the mind!

Photo 6-3

Photo 6-4

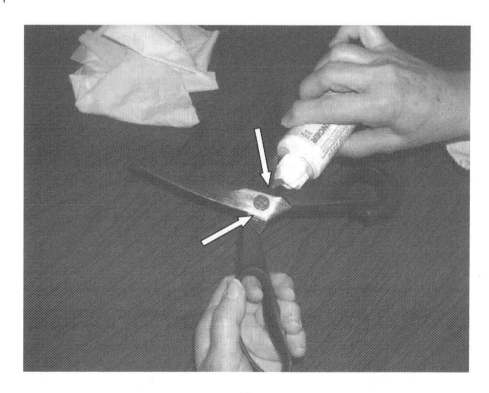

6-3) Tendency…While sewing, I see students place their scissors on the left side of the machine. As they remove the fabric from the machine their scissors go flying to the floor. Oh No!

The Problem….Not good! All sorts of things can get damaged. Scissors can nick the floor or carpet causing the scissor to get out of alignment. We have all done this because we cut the thread on the left side of the machines needle. However, it feels awkward reaching across oneself to puck-up the scissors. (Photo 6-3) Besides, your posture can suffer. There goes that nagging neck pain.

To Clarify………..To avoid the awkwardness: train yourself to rest your scissors on the right side of your machine. Also, when placing your scissors down make a <u>conscious</u> effort to completely close them. This will eliminate any chance of cutting something you hadn't planned on. The newer sewing machines have a cutter just to the left of the needle. However, I discovered this cutter does not cut both threads. "Oh, Bother". Now I <u>have</u> to pick-up my scissors to cut the ornery thread. Remember to set the scissors down completely closed and on the **right** side of the machine. Good habit to possess. When I say, "Completely closed", I mean it. You may inadvertently cut the cord to your sewing machine, what a shocking experience this could be. **A very important message to loved ones:** "He who takes my fabric scissors will experience my wrath". My family is still functioning normally, so they took me at my word and left my fabric scissors: ALONE!

6-4 Tendency…"Why are my scissors sticking? It is making them difficult to open and close."

The Problem….A dry hinge and the presence of lint both cause your scissors to act up. And heaven help the person who uses your fabric scissors to cut: *paper that has been glued!*
Did I get your attention?

To Clarify…….Metal rubbing against metal will cause your scissors to stick making it very difficult to operate. Take a moment to clean the lint off the blades – use <u>caution</u> because these blades are extremely sharp. Most of the lint you find on your scissors comes from fabrics with a pile such as: fleece; flannel, even velvet. After the blades are clean, open the scissors completely and apply <u>one drop</u> of *sewing machine oil*, **no substitutes**. (Drawing 6-4) Do this on both sides of the hinge. I even run a thin bead of oil along both blades. Now, open and close the scissors a multitude of times as you visit with the other students in the class. Use caution not to slam the scissors closed, this is very grading on the ear as well as the scissors. Wipe the oil off the blade with CARE. One time I did not pay attention and sliced my finger, ouch! After a while, you should notice the stiffness dissipates as you open and close your scissors. This action extends the life of your scissors when you follow a regular cleaning and oiling schedule. Have ready a cleaning rag, see top left corner of this photo 6-4. The Threads Magazine Issue #131, July 2007, page 14 shows a new Gingher scissor that will be a welcome relief for your thumb because of the invention of a shiny new spring release. It is about time they made cutting more user friendly. (See photo on following page.)

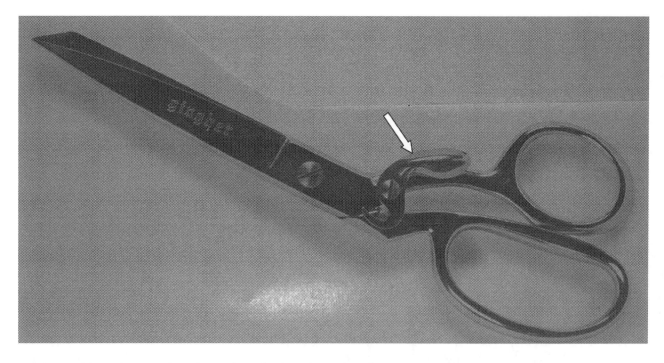

Pictured here is a product from the Gingher line with the spring action releasing mechanism.
Other manufactures have this feature as well. What a welcome relief for the thumb.
This spring action is on *regular sheers* as well as *pinkers*.
The lever is in gold (see arrow).

Section III

The Machine Parts

Preparing the Machine to Sew

Record Vital Information on Machines

Sewing Machine Make_____
        Model #_____
        Serial #_____
Warranty expiration date_____ *

~~~~~~

Sewing Machine Make_____
        Model #_____
        Serial #_____
Warranty expiration date_____ *

~~~~~~

Quilting Machine Make_____
        Model#_____
        Serial #_____
Warranty expiration date_____ *

~~~~~~

Serger Machine Make_____
        Model#_____
        Serial #_____
Warranty expiration date_____ *

~~~~~~

Embroidery Machine Make_____
        Model #_____
        Serial #_____
Warranty expiration date_____ *

* It is a good idea to put a sticker on your machine with the warranty expiration date written on it. This way you will know when to take your machine in for its last check-up before your machine warranty expires. Thanks Tassel!

#7   The Different Parts of the Sewing Machine

Drawing 7-1

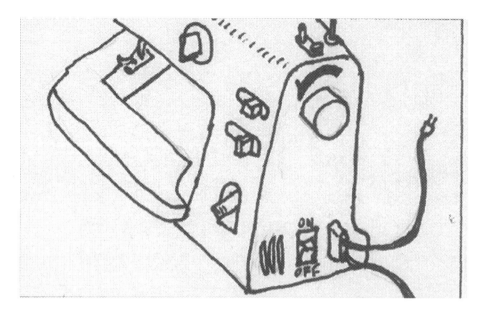

Observe the direction of the arrow.

Drawing 7-2 a, b, c, d

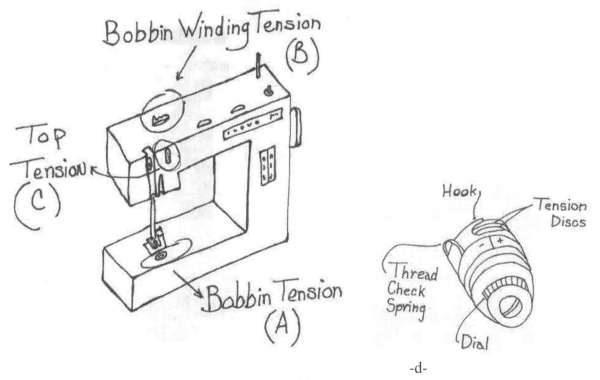

7-1) Tendency…Huge tendency! Students turning the hand wheel (flywheel) backwards, not good!

The Problem….When you turn the hand wheel backwards you confuse the sewing machine and could experience the course of the THREAD LOCK.

To Clarify……..You <u>must</u> turn the hand wheel forward, like a Waterfall. (Drawing 7-1) I can hear my students saying, "Waterfall, Waterfall", as they turn the hand wheel forward. Turning it the wrong way on a serging machine can really be bad. Note: there are a very few serging machines that operate in the reverse. Check your serger hand wheel (flywheel) to see which direction the arrow points. Some arrows point forward and others point towards the back. In the words of the information operator, "<u>Please</u> make a note of it!"

7-2) Tendency…Threading the machine through the *bobbin winding tension*.

The Problem…..As you thread the machine for sewing, slipping the thread through the bobbin winding tension will put unnecessary tension on the thread. Pretty soon the thread will break. Now you will have to rethread the machine and may cause the machine to be out of time. There goes another expensive trip to the sewing machine technician.

To Clarify……..There are three tensions on the sewing machine. Drawing 7-2a indicates where the bobbin case area is located. (Page 59 shows both types of bobbin case unites and their location.) The tension located on the top of the machine 7-2b is for bobbin winding, **only**. The tension on the front is used when threading the machine for sewing. Drawings 7-2c and 7-2d illustrates the two different styles of tension unites. Drawing 7-2c is tucked inside the machine. Some sewing and serging machines have the tension unit sticking out in front of the machine, 7-2d. [A word about which thread to use: generally we sew using the same thread from the same spool for bobbin as well as the top thread. Some times I have used different colored threads because of a time restraint. But this is not a good habit to cultivate. When using the *embroidery machines* use a special bobbin thread.]

Photo 7-3

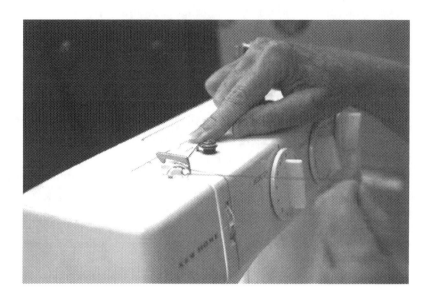

My right forefinger is to the right of the bobbin threading tension.
The thread is **not** in this tension.

Photo 7-4

I love my pin cushion   Looks like I need more coffee.

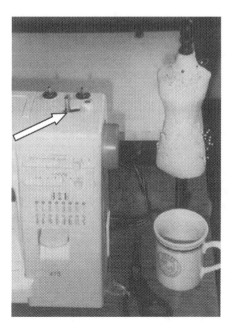 

7-3) Tendency…Not getting the thread firmly into the front part of the take-up lever.

The Problem…All sorts of mishaps can develop if the thread is not in the take-up lever. It is highly unlikely but possible to get the thread caught in the take-up lever shaft inside the machine. Oh No! This happened to a student of mine during class. My student said a prayer to guide my hands as I attempted to remove the thread wedged out of the working parts of the shaft. It took me many tries, using my *serger tweezers*, to get it untangled. I was successful: saving her gas money to deliver the machine to the repair shop; a hefty repair bill, and the worst part, not being able to use her machine for days on end.

To Clarify…….To avoid this, do the following: 1) as you pull the thread from the spool, place your finger of your right hand on the thread just to the left of the spool pin; 2) press gently against the top of the machine; 3) pulling thread with left hand, slide it under your right finger, using it as a tension guide, as you lead the thread down through the right slot where the tension is located; 4) then back up through the left slot and behind the take-up lever. At this point I tell my students to gently but firmly bring the thread around to the left and pull the thread towards them allowing it to slide firmly into the take-up-lever. (Photo 7-3) You will be able to watch the thread slide into the forward hole of the take-up lever. Wow, was that deep. One of my machines makes a snap sound telling me the thread is in the take-up lever. Next, remove your finger from the top of the machine and continue threading back down this same slot. There will be one or two more guides before you reach the needle. Just so you understand what I am talking about, remove thread and open up the left side hatch of your machine. You can either swing the door open, or take the screw out and remove the cover. Observe how the shaft moves as you turn the hand wheel, (Remember: Waterfall, Waterfall).

7-4) Tendency…"Where is the spindle (spool pin) for the thread?"

The Problem……If you cannot find a spindle to put your thread on, DO NOT use the bobbin winder spindle. (See arrow) For one thing the hole in the spool is to small to fit on the bobbin winder spindle. You will experience difficulty pushing the thread spool on it causing the thread to break because it won't spin. This spindle is for bobbin winding only.

To Clarify………Some sewing machines have one or two spindles on top that may be pushed down inside the machine. When getting ready to sew, pull the spindles all the way up. (Drawing 7-4) When transporting your machine to your class, push them down into the machine, left photo. The manufacturers designed the machine this way because there were numerous complaints when the spindles would brake off during transit. Other spindles are placed behind the motor housing. You will need to swing it away from the machine when sewing. Look all around, you will eventually find the spindle(s). Many of today's' sewing machines have horizontal spool pins. You must use the spool caps. Some caps have two discs: Singer made caps with both sizes on one cap. They fit the newer skinny thread spools as well as the traditional larger spools. Neither of these spool pins or caps mentioned here will fit the *cone thread spools* because the hole is much larger. They flop around as the sewing machine works causing drag on the thread creating bad stitches or even breaking the thread. The *cone spacer* will help keep your cone thread spools from flopping around. (See Photo 8-2 arrow on page 75.) As you improve your sewing skills there will be many more tools (toys) to enjoy.

Photo 7-5

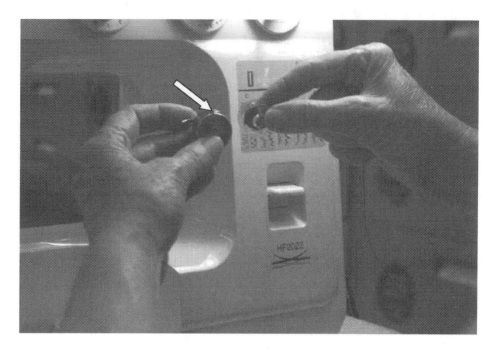

To use my method, hold your hands in this position.

Photo 7-6

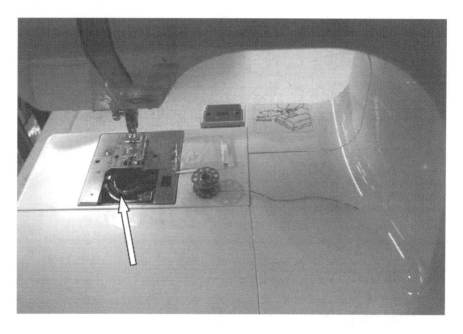

7-5) Tendency…"What on earth is a bobbin? And what is a front loading bobbin case? I have heard of a Shuttle bobbin do I need one?"

The Problem…..There is a huge assortment of bobbins on the market. If you use the wrong bobbin in the bobbin case you will experience problems with your seams, if you get a seam at all.

To Clarify……..Sewing machines work with two threads; a top and a bottom thread. The bottom thread is wound on a bobbin and works together with a bobbin case which has its own tension built-in. To prepare the bobbin, hold it with your thumb and forefinger of your <u>left hand</u>. (Not pictured) With your <u>right hand</u> pull the thread off the bobbin about three inches. The thread must be coming off the top of the bobbin. If not, flip the bobbin over 180°. With your right hand, curl your small finger and the one next to it and then the longest finger (three fingers in all) around the thread. Now transfer the bobbin to your <u>right thumb and forefinger</u> still holding the thread with your three fingers. (See Photo 7-5) After sewing for a while you will become ambidextrous using every finger on both hands: takes practice. Next, pick up the bobbin case with your left hand making sure the slot is at the top. (See arrow in Photo 7-5) Place the bobbin inside the case, slide the thread through the slot (should be on top) and gently snap the thread into the opening at the top of the bobbin case. Do not force the thread, it may break. To make sure the thread is in the tension correctly, hold the bobbin case on the outer circle, bobbin side up so it will not fall out: pull the thread. You should feel a gentle tug from the tension. A three inch thread tail is all you need when loading the bobbin case into the machine. Note: If you should be fortunate enough to own a Treadle Sewing Machine you will have a bobbin case in the general shape of a long bullet. It is called a shuttle bobbin. I own a working antique treadle sewing machine. How relaxing it is to rock my feet up and down as I sew. [A little known fact: the non electric treadle sewing machines are still manufactured today and shipped to areas of the world that have little or no electricity, like Belize.]

7-6) Tendency…"What is a drop-in bobbin.? Do I just willy-nilly drop the bobbin in?"

The Problem….Even though the bobbin drops into the built-in bobbin case, the sewing machine will not sew if you drop it in when the thread is going the wrong direction.
To Clarify……..Place the filled bobbin on the sewing surface of the machine. (Photo 7-6) Gently place your left forefinger on the bobbin and pull the thread off with your <u>right hand,</u> about three inches. As you look at the bobbin, ask yourself: is the thread coming off the front or the back of the bobbin. You want the thread to be coming off the front. If not, flip the bobbin 180°. Next slide the bobbin towards the built-in bobbin case keeping the thread tail to the right and drop the bobbin into the bobbin case. Hold the bobbin steady with <u>your right forefinger</u> and with the <u>left hand</u> take the thread and drag it towards the left. As you do this, watch the thread slide into the bobbin case tension slot. (See Photo 7-6 arrow) You may hear a soft snap. This indicated the thread is in the tension. At this point, remove your <u>right forefinger</u> and pull the thread towards the back with your <u>left hand</u> about a couple of inches more to insure the thread is in the tension correctly. Hay, that was easy! Next thing to do is to thread the machine and pull the bobbin thread up and you are ready to sew. (See Tendency 15-5 Page 117/8) Remember to check your stitch controls before you resume sewing.

Drawing 7-7

Drawing 7-8

MECHANICAL

COMPUTERIZED

SCREEN

TENSION

2 1
3 0
4
5

Length

ZIGZAG
WIDTH

⅛
¾

Stitch
Selector

¾

STITCHES

7-7) Tendency…Flicking the foot lever making the foot SLAM down on the feed teeth (feed dogs).

The Problem….You could damage the feed teeth, and the bottom of the foot, and the light weight fabric you are about to sew.

To Clarify……..I recommend getting a firm grip on the foot lever located either just above and behind the foot shaft or just to the right. On some serging machines you might find the foot lever clear over on the right side of the machine or just to the left of the needle shaft. Check your manual for the location. Now ease the lever down, SLOWLY. By being careful, the feed teeth will not make an imprint on the bottom of the foot (Drawing 7-7) or damage your more delicate fabrics. Every time I hear a student flick the foot down I cringe and say, "Ouch!" Pretty soon everyone develops the habit of easing down the foot.

7-8) Tendency…Lowering the needle before checking the width and stitch selector controls.

The Problem ….Try a test: with needle and foot in the up position change the width and stitch selector controls. Watch the needle bounce from side-to-side. If you have the needle in the fabric as you change the controls the needle could develop a permanent bend. This bent needle will damage the hook in the bobbin case: a very costly repair. Not to mention the time away from your sewing machine. Oh No!

To Clarify……..Should you own a machine that only sews a straight seam, than disregard this Tendency. But if your machine has two or more stitch selections, pay close attention to this one. It is beneficial for the needle to make any changes to your controls before you lower the needle into the fabric. Example: you have been sewing a zigzag and now you want to sew a straight seam. *Take a moment* to check the controls. (Drawing 7-8) If the needle is in the fabric, raise the needle, with the hand wheel (Waterfall, Waterfall, refer to Tendency 7-1, page 56) or use your needle up/down button. Now you can change the controls with certainty. Use caution when changing the control dials: 1) length of stitch; 2) zigzag width; 3) tension on the top thread; and 4) the pressure on the presser foot. A dashed line indicates length of stitch (the number of stitches to the inch, standard is about 2.5). Some machines have a toggle switch; others have numbers on a bar or a dial. A zigzagged line indicates how wide the stitch will be. It can be numbers or an actual zigzag line from the narrowest to the widest. Computer machine screens display numbers or plus and minus signs for length and width. The stitch selector control tells you what stitch the machine is ready to making: straight; blind-hem; decorative; et cetera. This could be push buttons, a dial or the touch screen images. Older machines have cams for the different stitches.

Photo 7-9

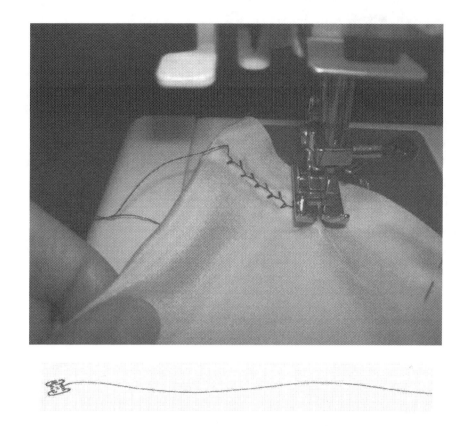

Drawing 7-10

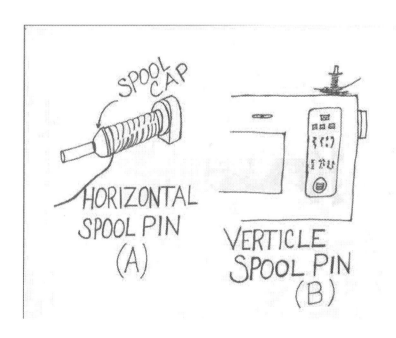

SPOOL CAP

HORIZONTAL SPOOL PIN (A)

VERTICLE SPOOL PIN (B)

7-9)Tendency…"Oops! That wasn't the stitch I wanted." (Photo 7-9)

The Problem…..You may be ripping out stitches if the machine is set to sew the elastic zigzag stitch when you wanted to sew a straight stitch. Those tiny stitches are a bear to rip out. Winnie the Pooh would say, "Oh, Bother".

To Clarify.........Before lowering the needle and foot, take that crucial moment, (the one I mention several times in this book) and glance at the controls. This look will confirm the stitch and width that your machine is programmed to make. Make any needed adjustments before you lower the needle and foot. If you forget to check the controls, take that moment to look at the stitches you just sewed. To do this: operate the machine for several stitches then stop sewing, put the needle down and raise the foot. Swing the fabric around far enough so you can see the stitches. Now you can determine whether the stitch is correct. (If you look behind the needle with the foot down, you will not be able to see the stitches. They are secretly hiding under the wide portion of the foot.) Swing the fabric back to sewing position and **lower the foot**. Continue sewing after you **lower the foot**. If, on the other hand, the stitch is not what you wanted, raise the needle and pull the fabric out. This way you won't have to rip out much. Nice save! Be sure the take-up lever is at its highest point: turn the hand wheel forward. Should the controls be set to what you want but the stitch is nothing like what it is supposed to be, your machine may need servicing. If the service call is too costly, another option would be to replace the machine. A word of caution when sewing machine shopping: unless you are sewing buddies do not take a friend with you to the store. Your non sewing friend does not know your sewing level. Why end a friendship!

7-10) Tendency…Thread spool is out of control, thread is everywhere.

The Problem …..Have you ever experienced your spool of thread flying off the horizontal spindle while sewing and then had to untangle the thread from everything it came in contact with? If you have a vertical spool pin and you are running the machine at lightening speed, you may skyrocket the spool to the moon. What fun your cat will have with the traveling thread spool. Another problem, when hitting the foot peddle suddenly or stopping suddenly the thread spool will spin out of control and the thread will whirl off the spool and get tangled around the spindle underneath the spool. Gasp! What a mess! (Drawing 7-10b) The thread gets tight instantly and breaks causing possible damage to the needle and more. Now we have to untangle the mess and possibly change the bent or broken needle. T i m e   w a s t e r !

To Clarify...........Everybody, SLOW DOWN! For the horizontal spindle there is a *thread spool cap* that comes to the rescue. (Drawing 7-10a) Not only does it keep the thread spool in tow, it helps the thread to come off the spool smoothly. Use the small cap for narrow spools and the larger cap for larger spools. For the vertical spindle a round flat *red felt pad* with a hole in it needs to be placed on the vertical spool pin and under the thread spool. This felt pad keeps the spool from jerking. If you do not have one, go directly to your sewing machine shop and buy one, they cost only pennies. You will find your stitching improves; the thread pulls off evenly, saving the needle from a premature death. Plus your machine will operate better. Remember to start pressing the foot peddle slowly as you reach the desired sewing speed. Then ease the speed down when stopping.

~~~~"Please make a note of it!"~~~~

Drawing 7-11

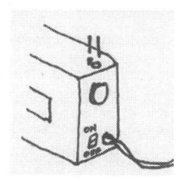

Drawing 7-12

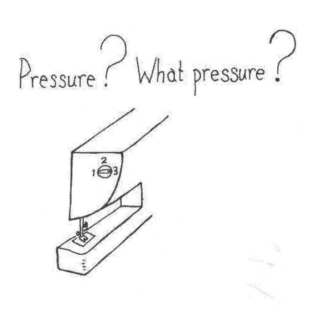

7-11) Tendency…"Teacher, why isn't my sewing machine running?"

The Problem……Safety features abound on today's serging and sewing machines. The foot peddle does not work when the light is off. In the past, too many cats sat on the foot peddle and burned out the motor. A bad smell you will not forget.

To Clarify……….There has been so many wonderful improvements done on the humble sewing machine. Our suggestions and complaints have been heard. As a sewing teacher, safety is one of my uppermost concerns. Today our sewing, serging, embroidery, and blind hem machines have many safety features. How nice! It is about time our concerns have been met! If you get no response while pressing the foot peddle, check the *on/off switch* located on the right side of the machine. (Drawing 7-11) It is a good practice to turn off the machine whenever you walk away from it. Also you might check the power cord to the machine and to the wall outlet to make sure there is complete contact. Once when I returned to my sewing machine, I unintentionally stepped on the foot peddle, Wow! An instant thread jam learned my lesson quickly. Besides, this cuts down on having to change your light bulb before its time. (See Photo on page 139)

7-12) Tendency…"What does this dial do?" "Pressure, what Pressure?"

The Problem…..The controls are confusing.

To Clarify………Your manual can help. A *Sewing Teacher* is better. When you purchase your machine at a reputable dealer, chances are they offer lessons on how-to operate your new machine. **Take this class as soon as you can. The benefits will be immediate.** Incase you did not, here is some help. For mechanical machines, the foot pressure dial is located on the left side of the machine or on top near the take-up lever. (Drawing 7-12) This dial you hardly ever need to change. It controls the <u>pressure</u> on the <u>presser</u> foot, the higher the number the greater the pressure. [Notice the different spelling of these words.] Some machines have a top indicator. It has a twisting knob and the higher the knob the lighter the pressure. Also, there may be a ring around the knob. When you press down on the ring, the knob jumps up: releasing the pressure on the presser foot. This allows you to sew free hand embroidery and mend. Ask your sewing teacher to show you how to mend with your machine using a hoop. These techniques are pretty slick. Confusing Huh? Hang in there: it gets easier with practice.

Drawing 7-13

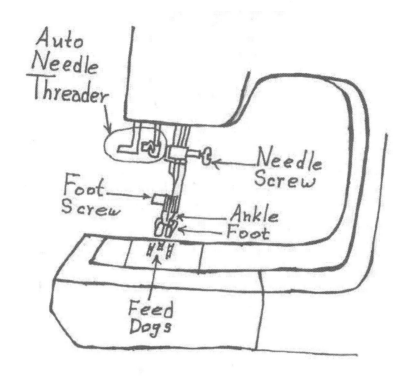

Photo 7-14

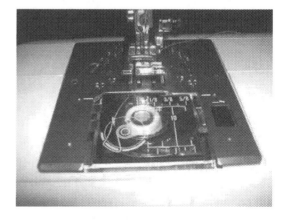

Notice the arrow pointing to the bobbin thread? If your thread is not in this position
it is <u>not</u> in the bobbin tension and you won't get a seam. Take that moment before continuing.

7-13) Tendency…"I do not know the sewing foot from the ankle nor the needle screw from the foot screw. Oh no, what happened to the serging needle screw? Help me, please!"

The Problem….*Foot/Ankle* - Years ago we had to loosen the foot screw to change the foot. Today's machines have been improved greatly: the feet now drop off the *ankle*. Oh No! How'd that happen? Truly this is a nice feature unless you don't know how to put the foot back on. *Foot Screw* - The foot screw can get loose after sewing for a while causing the foot to wiggle around or even fall off the post. *Needle Screw, sewing machine* - The needle screw can get loose, too. A worse problem is when changing the needle. Remember to toss after 8 to 10 hours of sewing. The needle can drop into the bobbin case area if you loosen the screw to much. This is where I get a queasy feeling. I know how difficult it is to remove the needle without damaging it or the bobbin case. Plus the needle screw housing can fall apart if you go too far. Caution: the serger inter workings posses an extreme challenge when removing a dropped needle. And the tiny needle screws are nearly impossible to find if they come out of their housing.

To Clarify........Here is the story: when you want to sew buttons, drop the all purpose foot off and snap the button foot on. Tendency 10-1, pages 87 shows how-to reattach the foot. Important rule-of-thumb: every once in a while take the screwdriver (the one that came with your machine but the screwdriver with the wings is better) and tighten the foot or ankle screw (**left side of the post**). Use your hand to tighten the screws then use the screwdriver to go just beyond hand tight: No More! Any tighter and you may need the assistance of your husband to change the foot. Use the previously mentioned process for the needle screw. Hold on to the needle (**left hand**) as you loosen the screw located on the **right side of the post**. [Note: Bernina feet are unique; therefore I stress that you take the free lessons when purchasing the Bernina sewing machine.] Check it out: there is a great tool to help you avoid any calamities: the *needle holder/inserter*, Tendency 2-10, page 17. The brush is pretty puny, but the opposite end has a tiny hole just the right size for your needle. The inserter will help you maneuver the needle through the tight area and prevent needle damage. For serging machines the needle area is extremely congested. The cost is minimal making this amazing tool a must have for your sewing basket. Suggestion: take a small mirror and hold it under the needle housing unit on the post before you insert the needle. You will see where the needle fits. For the serger, I leave the screw driver or *allen wrench* in the slot when replacing the needle and remove it only after the needle is secure. A word to the wise: in small increments, undo and tighten the needle screw(s) when removing and inserting your needles.

7-14) Tendency…When I first bought a sewing machine with a drop-in bobbin I kept forgetting to snap the plate back on and loosing it in the process. (Photo 7-14)

The Problem….As I guided the fabric to the foot I caused the bobbin to drag a little bit, OOPS!

To Clarify........After bringing up the bobbin thread via the needle, *take a moment* to snap the plate over the bobbin area. Now you are ready to sew provided you have all your dials the way you want them. Always something!

Photo 7-15

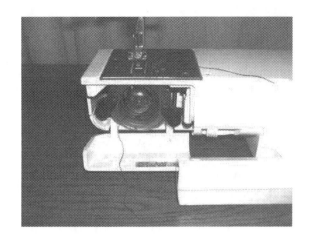 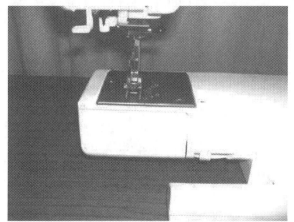

Drawing 7-16

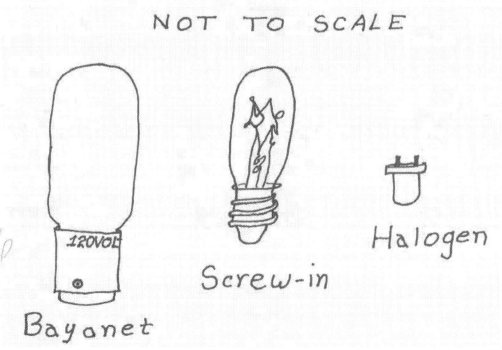

NOT TO SCALE

120VOL

Bayonet

Screw-in

Halogen

7-15) Tendency…"Why am I having trouble sliding the storage unit (sewing surface) back on to the machine?" (Photo 7-15)

The Problem…..You probably forgot to close the bobbin case area hatch of your front loading bobbin case machine. Do not force it, the plastic securing barbs on the storage unit may break off. The free arm is great while sewing sleeves or pant legs but you will miss the sewing surface for all the other sewing you will be doing, not to mention loosing your convenient storage unit.

To Clarify…...…Following the steps in this order: 1) after installing the front loading bobbin case 2) and after threading the machine 3) bring up the bobbin thread 4) <u>then</u> close the bobbin case area hatch. Next, replace the storage unit making sure it lines up properly as you slide it on the machine. When I follow this routine I know everything is complete and I am ready to sew. No more worries that I have forgotten something. Make a thoughtful effort to keep your storage unit close to your machine at all times. Can't tell you how many people loose this unit and finding a replacement is nearly impossible. I must admit when I started teaching sewing I had no conscious idea of what my hands were doing. I set out to trace my step-by-step motions I went through: my hands; fingers; arms and everything else. Wow, how is that for intensive training. 007 move over, I can handle it! Pay attention to the details and they will eventually become as automatic to you as they have with me.

7-16) Tendency…"When I go shopping for a light bulb the sales person asks, '…screw-in or bayonet style or halogen?' How can I tell? Too many choices."

The Problem…. Unless you have the bulb with you it is hard to say which one you need. (Drawing 7-16) Once-upon-a-time we had to use what ever auxiliary light was available: sunlight during the day only and at night candle and later incandescent light. This created dark spots. Later built in task lighting was developed. Wow! What a difference, only a little shadow in the needle area. For dozens of years we only had to contend with screw-in or bayonet style of bulbs. We had a 50/50 chance of purchasing the right bulb replacement. To add to the problem some sewing machines use an odd size. Now we have even more choices. Halogen lighting has come of age.

To Clarify….…..Today, some machines are equipped with two even three lights. Gee, I may not need my reading glasses. Well, maybe I better keep them handy. The easiest solution is to carry the bulb in your purse in the hopes that the fabric store or sewing machine store is on your list of things to do. If you are like me, the bulb will get lost in the bottom of your purse. Suggestion: it is popular today to make hand or shoulder bags. With your new or improved sewing skills you could design and sew special pockets and divisions into your purse to suite your lifestyle. What a fun project. I don't know about you but my purse is getting so large I may put wheels on it, but than I digress. Another thought would be to bring your *instruction manual* with you to the fabric or sewing machine store that is if you can find the book. But then this is way too logical?

Photo 7-17

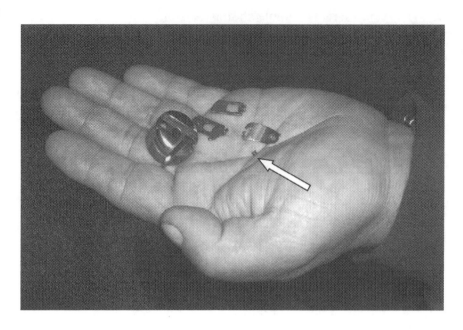

Drawing 7-18

-a-   -b-   -c-

7-17) Tendency…"Teacher, can you put this back together?" (Photo 7-17)

The Problem…."Oh you poor thing! There is nothing to do but send the bobbin case to its final resting place, in-other-words, the trash, sorry! Loosening the tension too fast caused it to fall apart.

To Clarify…......Occasionally a seam might not look right. The top and bobbin threads are not connecting between the layers of fabric correctly. Changing the bobbin case tension screw is risky business until you understand a "tiny" turn of the screw driver delivers an enormous difference in the tension spring. Going to far will cause the bobbin case to completely fall apart. To avoid this mishap I encourage my students to turn the bobbin case screw in dreadfully short increments. After each tiny turn of the screw driver, hold the thread and release the bobbin case. Gently "bob" the thread up and down. What you are looking for is to see the bobbin case drop slightly with each "bob". If the bobbin case drops to quickly then you have loosened the tension screw too far. Have your sewing teacher demonstrate how to adjust the bobbin case tension screw. See what the arrow is pointing to? Would you believe that is the tiny tension screw?

7-18) Tendency…Too often students quickly change the tension dial when the seam is not right.

The Problem …....If you see the bobbin thread on top (Drawing 7-18a) or the top thread on the bottom (got it?) then you are probably sewing with thin fabrics like *batiste*. Changing the top tension dial often can get confusing. You may develop a puckered seam if you tighten the tension too far. Another problem: if this tension is too tight the thread may break. If the top thread is too loose the thread will be floppy, or worse, the tension unit will fall apart. Not good!

To Clarify…........Here's help. The top tension has two discs tucked inside. When the foot is in the down position these discs are pressed together placing tension on the top thread. The top and bobbin tensions work together as you sew locking the two threads mid way between the two layers of fabric, this is good. If you are sewing very thin fabric with <u>regular thread</u> do not be alarmed when you see the seam looking like Drawing 7-18a, bad seam! It appears that the top or bobbin tensions need adjusting. So, before changing the tension you need to take into account the weight of the fabric you are sewing. For thin fabrics (like *chiffons*), I suggest sewing with *silk thread*. (Drawing 7-18b) Finding good quality silk thread is not easy but not impossible. Check the ads in your *Threads Magazines*. The two fabrics I mentioned above plus fabrics that stretch, including velvets, are difficult to handle for the beginner. Hold off buying these fabrics until you have more experience sewing. Drawing 7-18c shows how the seam looks when everything is working properly, good seam.

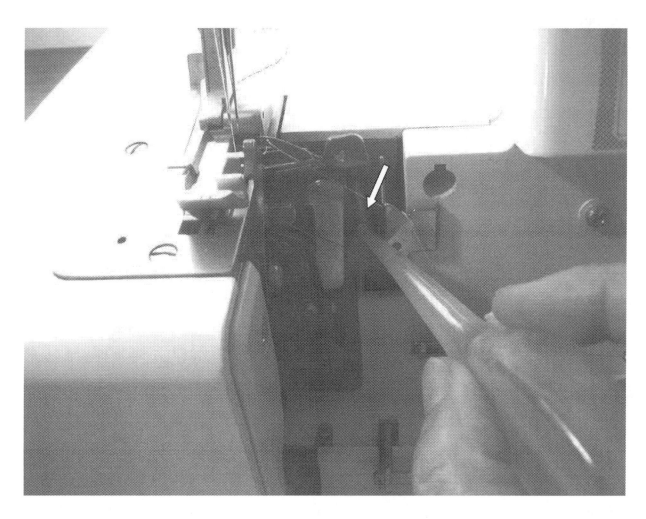

Oil your serger often, it only takes one drop.

This is the fine print: use sewing machine oil only.

#8 The Different Parts of the Serging Machine

8-1   I've had my serger for 2 years but I do not know how to thread it

8-2   Does the serger use a bobbin?

8-3   Can't I just buy a Serger if I do not have a sewing machine?

8-4   Just broke my serging machine and whacked my pin, H E L P !

Drawing 8-1

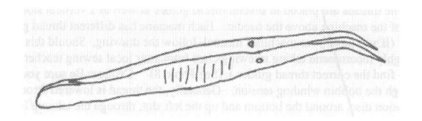

Photo 8-2

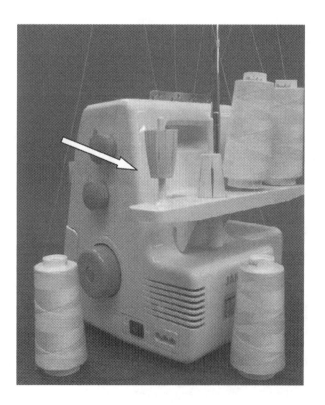

8-1) Tendency… "I've never used my serger. I've had it for 2 years but I do not know how to thread it and I do not want to use the four bright colored threads the machine came with."

The Problem…..Oh, what a shame! I know: it happened to me. Years later I **gave** my serger away. What a sad affair. It is common knowledge that you can tie the new color thread onto the one that is in the machine and this is OK. That is until the thread breaks. Now you are stuck because you do not know how to thread the machine. Believe me the thread can break.

To Clarify…….Well, you might as well bite the bullet and learn how to thread your serger. Or spend much more money and buy a Baby Lock that threads its self with air. Wow! What a great idea! But do not rest on your laurels, yet. It will still benefit you to take the <u>Learn to Thread Your Serging Machine Lesson:</u> within days after purchase. When you buy your serger at a reputable dealer the lessons should be part of the purchase price. If this is not an option, find an *independent sewing teacher*. **It is worth it to take a class on how to thread your serger,** there I said it again. In my classes I travel around the tables cutting the threads after everyone threads their machine. I hear my students groan! But then I follow up with, "Rethread your machines, I take no prisoners!" Oh, and see those really long *tweezers*? Use them! They will help you enormously. (Drawing 8-1) Once you learn the correct way to thread your serger, practice for about five minutes: **then go away**. When you have 5 minutes again, practice some more. **Only five minutes**, everyone can find five minutes. Do this many times until your fingers do it automatically. After your class and plenty of practice, you will understand the manual better and watching the video will make more since.

8-2) Tendency…"Now I know what a bobbin case is, but where does it go on my serging machine?" "There are so many threads, help!" "Do I have to learn to sew on the conventional sewing machine first?"

The Problem…"So many threads, so many questions, I will never get the hang of it. Where did you say the bobbin case goes?"

To Clarify…….Guess what, the serging machine does not have a bobbin case. Well, now you tell me. As a substitute, the machine uses four cone threads mounted on the back. To replace the bobbin there are two or three loopers (depending on how much money you are able to spend) located in the lower front part of the machine and behind a large horizontally hinged door. When using cone thread, pull the *cone spacers* off and reposition them upside down, they will keep the cones from flopping around. (Photo 8-2) You do not want <u>floppy cones</u>, the threads may get tangled up and break. Next, thread the machine in the correct order. A *savvy sewing teacher* will be a great asset in getting you started. To get the threads firmly in their respective tension disks use a dental floss action. Do not be surprised when your teacher comes along and cuts the threads. Oh, No! She is training you to thread your serger with every thread color change. No tying on the new color. It is not worth it in the long run. This goes double for the newer *Baby Lock Serge Machine* with its *threading by air system*. Go to the Baby Lock dealer and be dazzled with an **amazing** demonstration! After you learn to thread your serger, threading a regular sewing machine will be a cinch. Most people have learned on the sewing machine first, but try your hand on the serger. Men find the action on the serging machine fascinating.

Photo 8-3

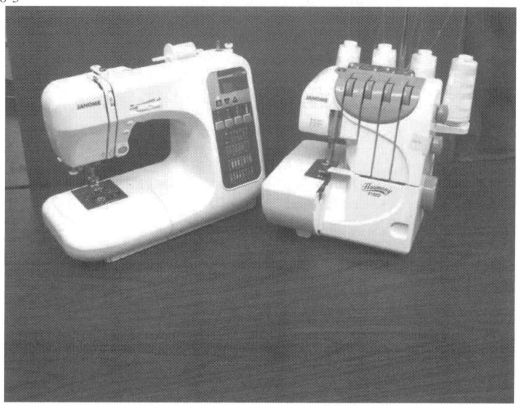

Photo 8-4

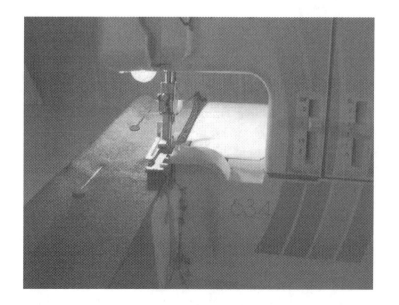

8-3endency…"Can't I just buy a Serger even if I do not have a sewing machine?"

The Problem…What if you need to make a buttonhole or sew an invisible zipper?

To Clarify……..First and foremost the serging machine is a <u>complement</u> to the sewing machine. It is really nice to have both machines, but not necessary. (Photo 8-3) After all, the home sewer only had sewing machines for about a hundred years. Overcastting the raw edge on the serger is superb. Sewing fleece and spandex is unrivaled. The serging machine is rapidly catching up to the sewing machine as far as the number of tasks the machine can handle. Gee, technology, isn't it wonderful? To think, a little over 100 years ago sewing was done exclusively by-hand.

8-4) Tendency…"Good golly! Miss Molly! I just broke my serging machine and whacked my pin in half."

The Problem…If you are using the long silk glass head pins the damage could be minimal. Should you be using thicker pins I guarantee you have just damaged the blades not to mention your fabric, the loopers, the thread and the pin you just destroyed. WOW, what a mess. And costly, too!

To Clarify……..Real simple: when serging two pieces of fabric together, go in about two inches from the cut edge and place the pins (about five inches apart) parallel to the edge you are about to serge. (Photo 8-4) This way you will not have to worry about pulling the pins out as you sew. But remember to pull them out when you finish serging. Use caution as the pins could catch your sleeves or dig into your skin. Not a pleasant feeling. Serging curves are a bit tricky. I do not use pins. Therefore, I suggest you serge a little slower and keep matching up the cut edges about 1 ½ to 2" ahead of the foot as you serge. Practice this: you will get the hang of it – but serge *slowly*.

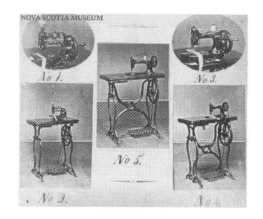

THE EVOLUTION OF THE SEWING MACHINE

Hand Crank Machine – powered by turning a crank with your right hand

Treadle Machine – powered by the feet you stand on

Mechanical Sewing Machine – powered by electricity

Almost Computerized Sewing Machine – powered by electronics

Computerized Sewing Machine – powered by small little chip(s)

Computerized Serging Machine – threaded by air

Long arm Quilting Machine – fabric is stationary, the machine moves

9 Power Cord and Foot Peddle

9-1   Power-cord/foot-peddle (PC/FP) unit has *disappeared*

9-2   Pulling the fabric as you sew on the sewing machine

9-3   Use your metatarsal arch to operate the foot-peddle

Photo 9-1

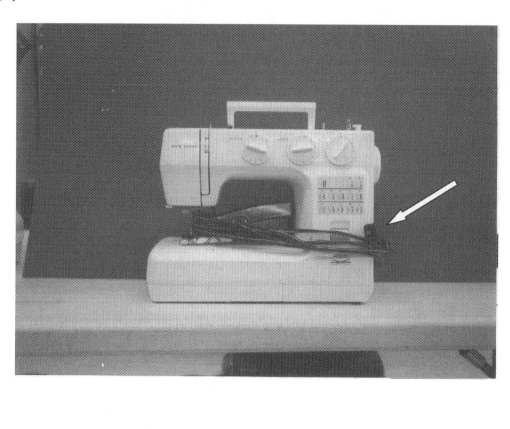

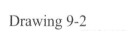

Drawing 9-2

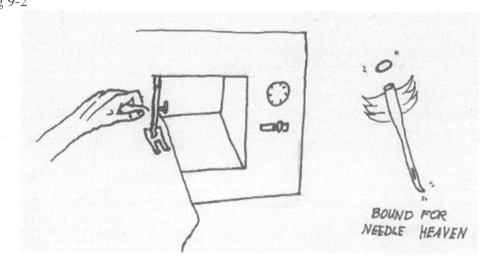

BOUND FOR
NEEDLE HEAVEN

9-1) Tendency… The disappearance of power-cord/foot-peddle units during a major move happens all too often. Also, can't tell you how many times my students bring their machines to class but leave their power-cord and/or foot-peddle at home. Rats! Not to worry, there are no idle hands in my classes: students hand sew or dream about their next sewing project.

The Problem….A misplaced cord too often becomes a lost cord. Unfortunately, we can not operate our machines without them, unless you have a treadle sewing machine. But then the treddle machine is too heavy and cumbersome to take to class.

To Clarify…..If you need to replace the PC/FP (power-cord/foot-peddle), find a reputable sewing machine dealer that will have the parts for your sewing machine model on hand. Bring the machine into the shop so the technician can locate the correct cords. This will save you time and several trips. In the future, avoid loosing your cords and all the running around totting your heavy machine to the repair shop: 1) place a small piece of fabric under the foot: 2) lower the needle into the fabric and lower the foot: 3) keep your cord plugged in to the machine: 4) wrap the cords together around the machine. Because you lowered the needle and foot you will not damage the cord as you wrap it around the needle post. As you get to the foot-peddle, slip it between the needle post and the motor housing. (Photo 9-1) Some of my students make a little bag to house their foot-peddle. This keeps it from scratching the machine. When you get to the plug, wrap it around the cord a couple of times. (See arrow) If your machine has a hard protective cover, you will have to unplug the PC/FP. Not to fret, make yourself a bag, slip the PC/FP unit into the bag and rest it on the sewing surface between the motor and the needle. See, there is always a way.

9-2) Tendency…Every new sewer demonstrates the tendency to place their left hand behind the needle grabbing the fabric they are sewing and setting themselves up to pull the fabric.

The Problem …This will damage the needle because you cannot push or pull the fabric thru the machine at the same speed the needle goes up & down. Period! (Drawing 9-2) Remember, you don't want to send your needle to needle heaven before its time!

To Clarify……..When preparing to sew, position your fingers at the front of your sewing machine surface. See Tendency 15-1, page 123 When your fingertips reach the foot, move your foot away from the foot-peddle (stop sewing) and reposition your fingers by bringing them back to the front edge of the machines sewing surface. Resume sewing. If you allow the machine to continue sewing a seam while one or both hands are off the fabric you will get a wobbly seam. Rats, more ripping. Note: some machines either come with a portable extended sewing surface or you can special order one to fit it; also having your machine in a cabinet presents a nice flat surface to prepare your fabric before it reaches the foot/needle area. Cabinets can be expensive. Years ago my husband took an old sofa table, cut a hole in it and fitted my sewing machine to it. He painted the table and a chair pink and gave it to me for my birthday. What a pleasure it was to sew on my new perfectly flush table. A natural next step was to I start my sewing business that year. A hint from Stephnie: I trained myself to automatically move my foot away from the foot-peddle when I lift my hands from the fabric piece I am sewing. This action can improve your eye-hand-foot coordination and avoid ripping out any wobbly seams. Comes with practice! Later after you gain more confidence in yourself, you can do what is called "taught" sewing.

Drawing 9-3

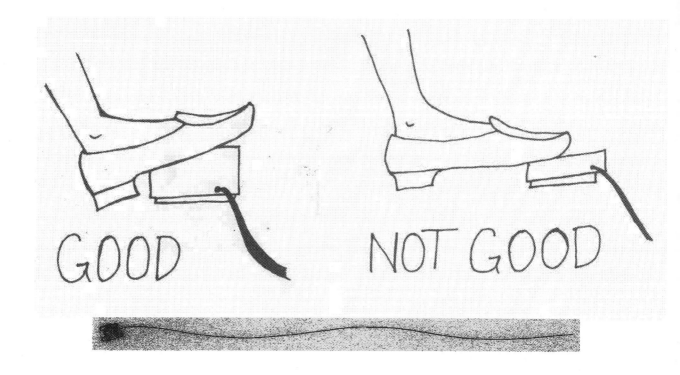

9-3) Tendency…I hear buzzing, and then, sewing machines running too fast.

The Problem …Speaking only to women and those of us that drive, we actually use our toes on the accelerator in our automobiles. Can you relate? After driving for a while we experience pain traveling up our shinbone. The same goes for sewing.

To Clarify……..There will be less fatigue if you use your *metatarsal arch* to operate the foot peddle. (Drawing 9-3) Slide your foot up on the foot-peddle to the highest point. This way you will have better contact, better control and exert far less force as you push down on the foot-peddle. The motor runs smoothly instead of jerking. An added benefit is that you won't buzz your motor. Mighty hard on your sewing machines motor not to mention the teacher's ear!

"Next,

    put your

        foot down.

           No,

                not the one

                    you are

                        standing on!"

#10 Feet, not the ones you stand on!

10-1   How did the foot come off? How does it get back on?

10-2   Rats, I just sewed the entire seam and there is no thread.

10-3   I can sew a button with my sewing machine?

10-4   What is a zipper foot and how is it used? Do I have a zipper foot?

10-5   Many sewers do not know how to use the wide assortment of feet.

Photo 10-1

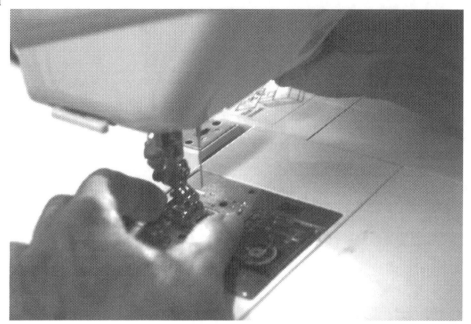

Photo 10-2

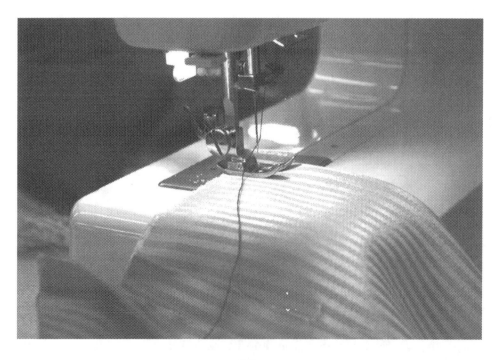

10-1) Tendency…"How did the foot come off? More importantly, how does it get back on?"

The Problem …...Oops! You probably triggered the lever or button behind the foot. Every time you push it towards you the foot will fall off. As Winnie the Pooh would say, "Oh, Bother"

To Clarify……...To snap the foot back onto the ankle, it is better to rest the foot on the feed dogs. To keep control of the foot as you connect it to the ankle, hold the foot with your left forefinger and thumb moving it just a little bit (forward or back) at the same time placing your right hand *firmly* on the foot-lever and <u>easing</u> down the ankle. (Photo 10-2) A solid grip on the foot with the thumb and finger will help you line up the bar on the foot with the opening on the ankle. You may hear a snap sound. Congratulations! You have successfully attached the foot to the ankle. Wasn't that easy? When you get ready to change the feet (not the ones you are standing on) replacing feet will be quicker than the old fashion way. Personally, I like the snap on feet much better. *Bernina* has the best foot unit made today. It slips on and off easily and aids the sewer with superior results. So, go see a demonstration, it will be worth your time.

10-2) Tendency…."Rats, I just sewed the entire seam and there is <u>no</u> seam, just needle holes." "When did I run out of bobbin thread?"

The Problem ……When the thread is left above the foot, (Photo 10-2), chances are the thread will be pulled out of the needle by the take-up lever as you take that first stitch. Pretty soon you will realize that you have sewed the entire seam without thread. (Some fabrics, like satin, will leave needle holes. Satin fabric is not forgiving.) Front loading bobbins can be a mystery all on their own.

To Clarify……... Before you place your fabric under the foot, you need to route both top and bottom threads under the foot and towards the back of the machine. I have trained myself to lower the needle into the fabric precisely where I want the seam to start. Occasionally I will catch myself lowering the needle and the foot and forget to place the top thread under the foot. I *take a moment* to lift the foot and ease the top thread under the foot towards the back of the machine. Should you have laps of preparedness, check the finished seam after sewing about three inches. For the front loading bobbin sewing machines it is not convenient to check how much thread remains in the bobbin unless you take the whole unit out. Therefore, look at the bobbin or bottom thread every once in a while. This will alert you when the bobbin thread has run out, another time saver. Sometimes I can hear a change in sound when this happens. The drip-in bobbin is visible so you can see how much thread remains by lifting up the fabric in front. Remember, you will avoid wasting precious time by taking that <u>important moment</u>.

Drawing 10-3

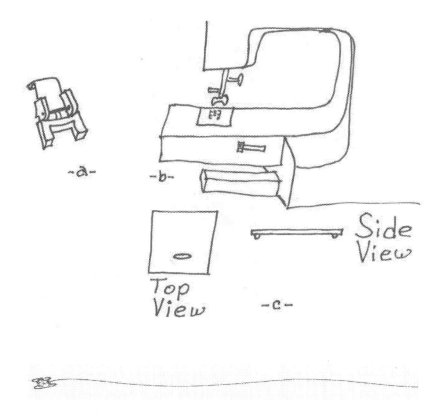

-a-   -b-

Top
View

Side
View

-c-

Photo 10-4

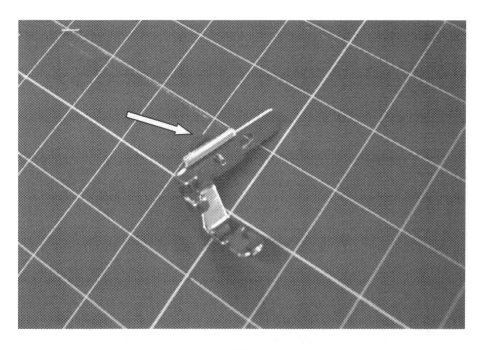

10-3) Tendency…"I can sew a button with my sewing machine?"

The Problem …..You can, but use caution! You do not want the feed dogs (teeth) to move the fabric and button causing the needle to hit the button sending the needle to needle heaven and the button to button heaven.

To Clarify...........Your zig-zag sewing machine can sew buttons; however, you must cover up or lower the feed teeth, first. Drawing 10-3a is the snub nose foot for sewing buttons on (my "toes" happen to be blue). I do not recommend you take the *stitch length* to O when sewing buttons on. Some sewing machines have a built in lever to lower the feed teeth. This lever can be in one of three locations around the bobbin case area: 1) at the back; 2) in front behind the bobbin case hatch, removing the accessory tray first (Drawing 10-3b); or 3) on the left side. Check your manual as to which way to move the lever. I own nine sewing machines which means I have to look in all three areas to find the spot where the lever is located. Wouldn't you know: each one is different! If you find no lever to lower the feed teeth there should be a plate in your accessory tray to snap over the feed teeth. (Drawing 10-3c) Just to keep me on my toes, one of my machines uses the plate that snaps over the teeth. Again check your manual. A sewing teacher can help you learn how to sew buttons on with your sewing machine. A button sewed this way is more secure then sewing it on by-hand. An additional task you can do when covering or lowering the feed teeth is free motion work like quilting, monogramming, and embroidery work using a hoop. Try it with the help of a sewing teacher. It is really exciting all the things you can accomplish on the sewing machine.

10-4) Tendency…"What is a zipper foot and do I have to used it?"

The Problem ….. When using a regular *all-purpose foot* for sewing zippers and piping you will not be able to get the needle close enough to the teeth (zipper) or the cord (piping) to be successful. Piping? What is that for?

To Clarify..........Many new sewers do not realize there are several wonderful feet that make sewing tasks more efficient and easier to handle. The old fashion *zipper foot* has an adjustable bar with a screw (arrow points to a red knob) at the back of the foot and two half moon cutouts where it rests on the feed teeth. (Photo10-4) I find this foot much more efficient then the one that comes with the new sewing machines. So, remember, by taking sewing lessons you can learn how easy it is to sew a zipper with the zipper foot. There are several ways of installing a zipper: inside pockets; the French Fly Front; in seam – invisible; lap over; pillows and cushions; purse closure; even cargo pants pockets. Practice the standard installation on flat fabric until you feel confident, then go for the more fun zippers. (See Photo 3-4 page 25) Piping is used in pillows, upholstery, table cloths even in clothing. The last time I made a Mandarin collar I enhanced it by sewing a small piping around the top edge. It looked great and helped to hold the collar up.

Photo10-5

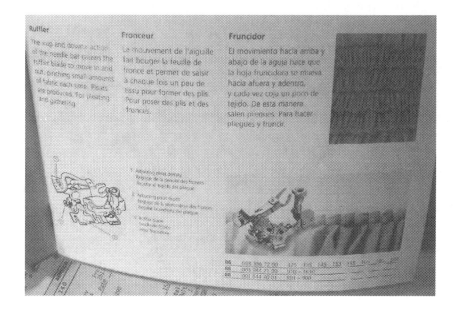

Photo 10-5a

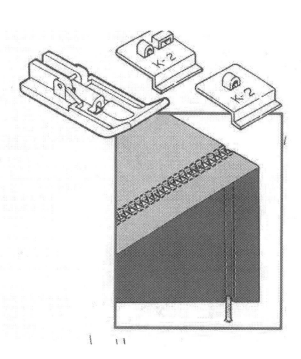

A trapunto effect is achieved when the cover hem stitch, pintuck foot and cording guide are used together. The corded pintuck works well on medium weight and knit fabrics.

1. Select sewing program: Cover Hem
   Thread and set up machine as indicated on display screen.
   Attach pintuck foot K.
2. Insert cord or yarn through groove on cording guide K-2. Open left side door.
   Set notch on cording guide into needle plate hole, close left side door.
3. Position cord under pintuck foot groove. Leave a 5 cm (2") tail behind foot.
   See figure 1.
4. Lay fabric (right side up) on top of cord and under presser foot. Lower needles into fabric. Lower presser foot.
5. Sew first two stitches by hand turning the flywheel. Continue sewing at a medium speed. See figure 2.

HINT: Wrap the cord or yarn end with clear tape for easy insertion into the K-2 guide.

NOTE: See PRO Card A2 – Cover Hem Tuck K2

En utilisant l'ourlet couvert, le pied nervures et le guide à mèche on obtient un effet Trapunto.

1. Sélectionner le programme de couture: Ourlet Couvert.
   Enfiler et préparer la machine comme indiqué sur l'écran.
   Fixer le pied nervures K.
2. Insérer la mèche dans le guide K-2. Ouvrir le couvercle de côté.
   Placer le téton du guide dans le trou de la plaque aiguille. Fermer le couvercle.

10-5) Tendency…Several feet come with your sewing and serging machine purchase. However many sewers do not know how to use them.

The Problem….You will waste time and energy. So, get out your different feet (no, not the ones you stand on) and learn to use them.

TO Clarify…… There are many more feet available at your reputable sewing machine dealer or on-line. *Nancy's Notions* is a great web site. Each time you use your sewing machine feet your tasks become easier, more efficient and save time. One of the largest sewing machine feet is called the *ruffler*, (Photo 10-5a). This is one of the very first feet to be invented and it looks pretty much like it did from the beginning (cir: late 1800's). Once you understand the intricate workings, you can make yards and yards of ruffles in practically no time. If you are interested in making tons of ruffles, then this is a must have foot for you. For this photo, my friend loaned her Bernina Foot Book. She mentioned that every time she picks up the book she is encouraged to use the different feet. As you can see, the drawings and text are excellent.

I happen to own an *Elna Serging* Machine. I purchased a few specialty feet and the instruction book to go with them: a valuable purchase because the drawings and text are easy to understand. (Photo 10-5b) I do recommend taking lessons. Your teacher can help you with the techniques. When you start using your feet your garments start taking on a really special and professional look. Everyone will be asking you where you bought that great outfit. I usually smile and say: "I made it!"

A word about sewing and serging machine *work books*: purchase the work book to go with your new sewing and serging machines. This can aide you and your sewing teacher to better understand your machine.

Notes:

Posture

Irons

Hand Sewing

Oh! My Aching Back!

#11 Posture, Not That Again!

Photo 11-1

Oh, my aching shoulders and neck.

Ahhhh! Much better!

Drawing 11-2

11-1) Tendency…."Oh, my aching back! And my neck is stiff!"

The Problem ……I can't tell you how many times I hear "My back hurts when I…"

To Clarify… …… Mine did too until I started sitting correctly in front of my sewing machine. What a simple solution to a nagging back pain. Here is how we do it at Sew Pros: sit down in front of your machine, put your chin to your chest and, with out lifting your chin, raise your eyes and look at the needle. Are you looking <u>directly</u> at the needle? No cheating! Look straight ahead. Every time my students do this I hear the chairs moving and a little giggling as they reposition themselves directly in front of the needle. Once this short exercise is complete, a sigh usually follows and everyone's awkward position melts away. Good *posture* is fundamentally important if you want to avoid future backaches. (Photo 11-1) Notice in the left photo: only my toes are on the foot peddle (see arrow). I am hunched over <u>and</u> I am seated way forward in the chair. Unfortunately this is how many of us look while sewing. The right photo shows my metatarsal arch way up on the foot peddle (see arrow). I am sitting square in front of the needle. My "tussah" is all the way to the back of the chair seat: this way my Lumbar region has plenty of support. Once my students are sitting correctly, I tell them to keep their head level, back straight and look <u>down</u> with their eyes towards the needle area. No more bunching shoulders and back pain. Your back and neck will thank you. Speaking of your back, try this the next time you sit in front of your computer. While using these simple posture techniques, writing <u>Sewing Doesn't Have to be a Mystery</u> proved to be a much less exhausting venture.

11-2) Tendency…I see students leaving there pinky finger out of the larger finger hole of their *bent handled scissors* or squeezing all four fingers in the larger hole, Ouch! My Students say, "But my pinky finger gets in the way so I leave it out."

The Problem……Your pinky finger <u>does</u> get in the way. Then again the act of opening and closing the *scissors* with all fingers inside can be limiting and difficult. What's more you could develop a cramp in your hand. Rats, which one is the lesser of two evils?

To Clarify..……..Neither! You will get a better cut if you place your pinky finger inside the larger finger hole. Well gosh! Now you have too many fingers inside the finger hole. Not to worry, take a look at your scissors. You should see a dent at the top outside rim of the larger finger hole. (Drawing11-2, see the arrow) This is where your index finger goes. Now your remaining three fingers will fit nicely in the larger finger hole. Instead of short choppy and many times jagged cuts you can open and close the scissors with ease and make a longer and smoother cut. This will take some practice, but it will be worth it later on. Take your *paper scissors* and practice cutting paper you were planning to toss out. Did you notice I said "paper scissors"? Woven and knit **fabrics** are to be cut using your good *bent handled shears*, ONLY! Fabrics like shinny dots that have been glued on will play havoc with your good shears. Therefore, use your recently sharpened paper scissors for that cutting job. Be sure to clean the scissors when you are done and use caution, they are very sharp. Rubbing alcohol with a thick cloth works well. Leave your good shears for cutting wools, fine cottons, Rayon's, silks and other quality fabrics. A word on cutting out your pattern: Cut today and sew tomorrow. I find my back will not hurt as I start sewing when I follow this basic rule. And, DO NOT hurry! Mistakes happen!

Photo 11-3

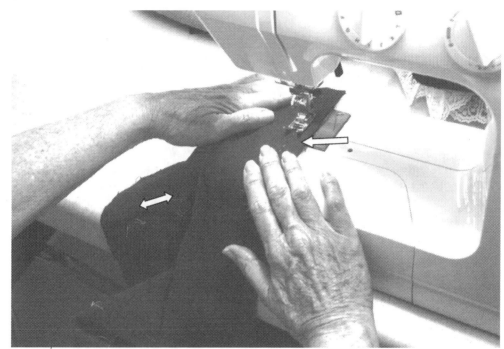

Note the *basting* and *tailors tacks* in the piece being sewed.

11-3) Tendency....I see so many students resting their arms on the table and their wrists on the machine.

The Problem......When <u>manual</u> typewriters were the only game in town, we learned to curve our fingers and keep our wrists elevated in order to make solid contact on the keys. This gave us the power to strike the keys as our fingers traveled downward. And then the IBM Selectric arrived, making lazy typists' of us all because we did not need to exert such power. I see many people at the computer almost lounging leaving their wrists on a pad and striking the keys at an angle instead of striking the key in the center. After a while the keys start sticking. NOT GOOD! Meanwhile back at the sewing machine..... Unfortunately, this same posture has come to the sewing machine. (Photo 11-3) A flat heavy hand, a thumb pushing against the front of the machine, arms leaning on the table all hinder the fabric from moving under the foot properly. These actions make your sewing machine work too hard. And eventually the needle will bend or break. Even if you work with a computerized sewing machine you must not adapt these bad habits developed from using the PC's of today. Oh, my gosh! What am I to do?

To Clarify.........By using good posture and raising your elbows up slightly, you will not be tempted to lean. What I recommend is to sit with your back straight and your head at a natural level; then look down at the machine. You will find this posture makes it convenient to sew relaxed for a longer period as long as you take mini breaks about every twenty to thirty minutes. When I attended the University of Hawaii, my physics professor suggested I follow the twenty or thirty minute timeline while studying. It works. Good posture really is important. Note: you might consider transferring these good posture techniques to your PC. The keys will not stick and you will feel better physically after hours at the screen. For the record, I kept my fingers curved while writing this book on the PC: the fatigue factor just did not exist. No brag, just fact! No carpal tunnel syndrome for me, thank you very much.

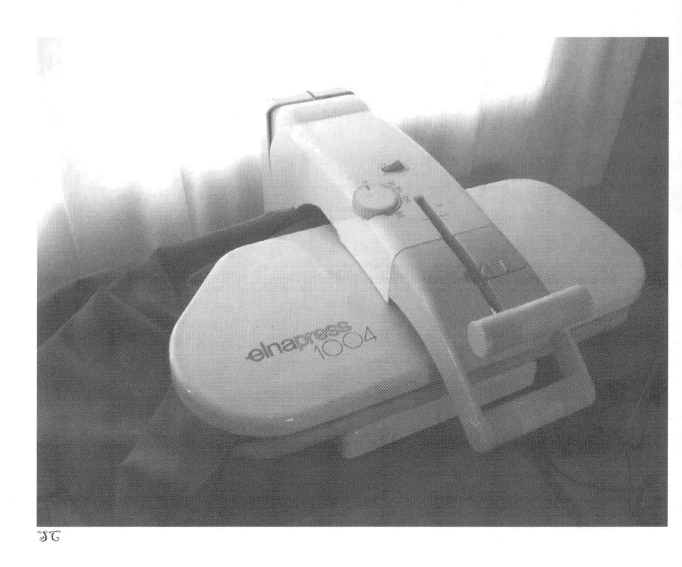

My home press makes great creases in slacks!

#12   Steam or Dry Iron, Yes You Need One

Drawing 12-1

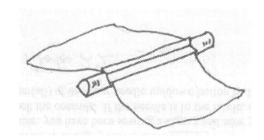

Photo 12-2

12-1) Tendency…Using a naked iron, how indecent.

The Problem ….. Many fabrics do not like a bare iron, ex: Fleece, Spandex, and wool. Using an unprotected iron on the right side of fabrics and finished garments can damage the fibers. The yarns that make up the fabric will: becoming fused together; loose its texture, and will develop a shine. That is enough to encourage anyone to toss their iron out on its ear.

To Clarify…..….Don't do it! After you sew a seam, *steam press* it open on the inside of the garment using a *pressing log* (Drawing 12-1) as well as a *soft thin press cloth,* see photo on page 27. You can purchase a press cloth at any notions/fabric store or on line. Some Polyester/Cotton blend fabrics will work well without a press cloth. But to be sure, test the bare iron to determine whether to use the press cloth or not. Some thinner fabrics sewed on the *serging machine* can be pressed to one side, usually towards the back at the shoulder and side seams. Fabrics such as fleece and Spandex are best <u>not</u> ironed. Check your pattern instruction to see which way to press the different seam allowances. Example: when sewing the cuff onto the sleeve, press the seam allowance towards the cuff. If you need to press the finished garment on the right side, use the press cloth or an *iron* that has a *protective coating*.

12-2) Tendency…"Oh no, I just scorched my fabric."

The Problem…...The student, before you, may have been pressing linen fabric which needs a very hot iron. (Photo 12-2) You come along with your polyester fabric and, *TOO HOT*! *Ouch!* You just scorched your fabric. If you do not have extra fabric to replace the damaged piece, problems abound. It is tempting to toss out your sewing project. But not in my class: we just get creative. This is when sewing becomes a wonderful extension of your abilities. Go for it!

To Clarify…..….In a class room situation it is always an excellent idea to check the temperature of the iron before pressing. Should you damage your fabric, a trip to the fabric store to purchase more fabric may be fruitless if your fabric is sold out. Gee, it only takes a moment to check the irons temperature gauge. You know the phrase, "Look before you leap"? It will save you time, money and disappointments. Some sewers purchase more fabric than needed just for an emergency like this. Not a bad idea unless the price tag is high.

Drawing 12-3

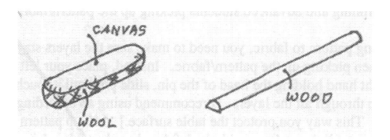

Photo 12-3

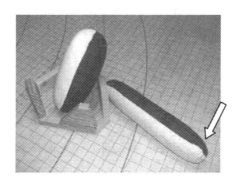

Photo 12-4

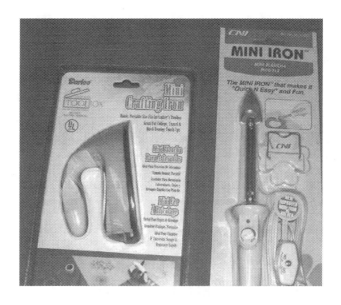

12-3) Tendency...."What do I have to press?"

The Problem......Sewing across another seam without pressing it open could get very bumpy and the finished garment will be uncomfortable to wear.

To Clarify..........Sewing a seam across another seam needs to be smooth and flat. To do this you need to press the seam open (example: the skirt side seam at the waist band area). To help you open the seam out and make it flat, I recommend using a *wooden press log* for long seams or the fabric covered *padded pressing log* for shorter seams. (Drawing 12-3) The latter is covered on one side with wool fabric the opposite with canvas. The canvas side is used when the iron needs to be set on very high heat. Use these tools to avoid ridges along the seam line. The right side of our garment will appear nice and flat. Straight seams are fairly easy to press open. I use one hand to open up the SA (seam allowance) while my other hand moves the iron towards the left hand. Be careful to move your hand holding the iron at the same speed as you separate the SA with your other hand. Developing the eye-hand coordination is a must to keep from searing your hand. Use the full length of the irons sole (flat surface) while it slides from one end of the seam to the other end. The tip of your iron travels down the center of the SA. No fishtailing, see page 105. Darts are another story. Most of the time darts can be pressed to one side. Front and back darts in a skirt are usually pressed towards the side seam. Placing the tip of the dart at the rounded end of the padded press log (see arrow) will help you press the dart smoothly and avoid unwanted creases at the tip. (Photo 12-3 shows the Tailors Ham resting in a convenient wooden holder, helps free up your hands to handle the fabric.) If your fabric is thick, like wool, cut the dart on the fold line. Do not cut all the way: stop about ½" from the point. Lay the fabric on the *padded pressing log* with the tip of the dart at the rounded end spread open the dart like a seam. The ½" part will resemble a triangle. If you have a *tailors ham* this works even better. I recommend purchasing the pressing log first. Maybe put the Tailors ham on your personal gift list. When pressing be sure you use the entire length of your irons surface. This way you have thoroughly pressed the seam open.

12-4) Tendency...Beginners do not realize how important the iron is during the sewing process.

The Problem....Your finished sewing project will not look good because the seam areas are not smooth and flat. When you get ready to press your garment you may be creating pleats where the seams are.

To Clarify........Here are some fabric exceptions that you should not press: fleece, Spandex, glued on sparkles, et cetera. The ironing tools available today are pretty amazing; iron covers, special ironing board covers and treated sole plates. The quilters really like the irons in the Photo 12-4. Because they are so tiny, it makes pressing their tiny pieces much easier. *Darico Mini Crafting Iron* and *Clover Mini Iron* are just a few products available on-line or at your favorite fabric store.

Drawing 12-5

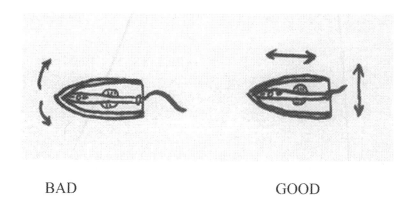

BAD   GOOD

12-5) Tendency…Fishtailing your *iron.*

The Problem…...When ironing, most people fan the tip of the iron in an arch, this is called fishtailing. (Drawing 12-5) As a result you are pressing the fabric on the bias and can stretch it out of shape.

To Clarify...……A more efficient may to press is to move the *iron* forward and back and side-to-side. I actually use the *iron* and *ironing board* more then my sewing machine. 1) Many times the fabric comes out of the washing machine wrinkled. Press the wrong side. 2) After sewing a seam, press it flat. This "sets" the stitch. 3) Then press it open or to one side according to the pattern instructions. Pressing a SA open makes it smooth and flat. No fishtailing, please. Sometimes I will use the *finger* press technique for thin fabrics as a temporary press while at the sewing machines. When sewing areas like cuffs, you will be pressing the SA towards the cuff. Check out the article on *irons* in the Threads Magazine issue #128, Dec/Jan 2007, pages 60 – 65. I believe you will find the answers to: "which one of these things do I need" question. My preference is not to use steam when pressing my sewing projects. Instead, I use a dry iron and place a damp cloth on the fabric. This works well for me. The other day while chopping for a new iron, I discovered the old style iron like I used to have only it was brand new. Right then and there I decided to purchase it just because it did not have all the currently popular bells and whistles that never seam to work right. Do your homework and purchase what soot's your ironing needs.

Drawing of a professional seamstress from a photo

in Couture Sewing, by Claire Shaeffer

13 Of course We Do Hand Sewing From Time To Time!

-108-

Drawing 13-1

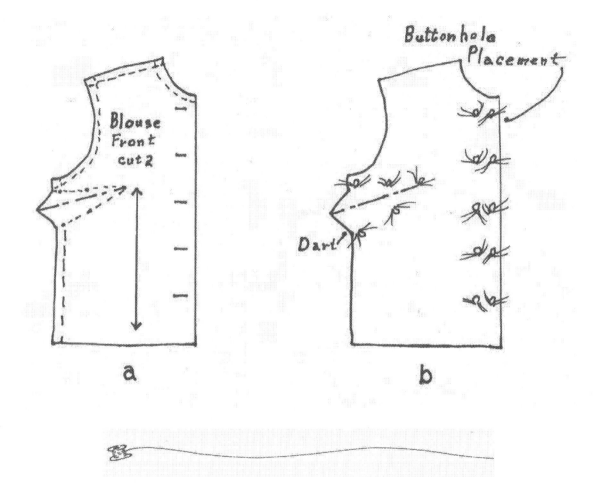

Blouse
Front
cut 2

Buttonhole
Placement

Dart

a

b

Drawing 13-2

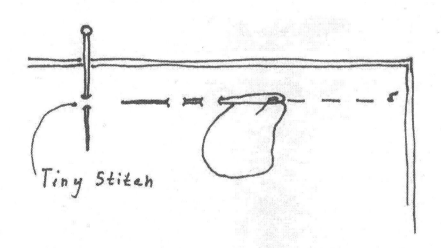

Tiny Stitch

13-1) Tendency…Loosing the mark (pins or chalk) before sewing.

The Problem….Another time waster: either guess where the marks are or dig out the pattern piece again, lay it on the fabric and remark each dot. (Drawing 13-1a)

To Clarify……..Some patterns have many dots, squares, and triangles indicating the location of buttonholes and buttons, pockets, special starting or ending points in the seam and etcetera. Most of the time I mark these indicators with *tailors tacks*. Where the triangles are along the cutting lines, I sew a running stitch by hand about three or four stitches perpendicular to the cut edge. To make the tailors tack, I cut a very long thread about two yards long. *Waxing* the thread will help it from getting tangled. Thread the needle. The cut ends need to be of equal lengths. No knot is needed. With the tissue pattern still pinned to the fabric, take the needle and scratch a small hole in the tissue at the "dot". Make a "tiny stitch" with the needle in the fabric. To make this process less cumbersome do the following: pull the double thread about 12 inches and lay the needle down; place one hand next to the pattern/fabric where you made the "tiny stitch"; with the other hand, pull the double thread stopping just before you reach the thread ends about 1-1/4 inch. Make a second "tine stitch" cross wise. Pull the threads in the same fashion. But this time stop when you make a loop smaller than the thread ends: but not to tiny. (Drawing 13-1b) Cut the thread. When all the tailors' tacks are complete, very carefully pull the tissue pattern away because you may have caught a little bit of the tissue in the stitch. Next pull the two fabrics slightly apart, enough to snip the threads. The Tailors Tacks are so cute plus they will not come out of the fabric. I found in my stash a wool jacket I started a couple years ago and only got as for as the Tailors Tacks. I was so pleased they were still there: finished the jacket in three days.

13-2) Tendency…Beginning sewers think basting by hand takes too much time. (Drawing 13-2) Basting by machine is faster, but…

To Clarify……..I personally do not like to baste a seam by machine. I feel the machine is working the fabric too much: what with moving feed dogs and pressure from the presser foot.

The Solution….In some places basting by hand is diffidently beneficial. However, I do not encourage my students to baste in the beginning. I hold off until they start the real intricate sewing projects, like: patch pockets, vents in jacket sleeves, you know, tailoring stuff. Teaching my students how to sew hems by hand, buttons with shanks, etcetera is more productive in the beginning. You would be surprised how quickly a beginner can ease into the more intricate tailoring techniques. Or not, no pressure here, learn at your pace. The nice part of *Tailors Tacks* and *basting* is that you can see your marks on both sides of the fabric.

Drawing 13-3

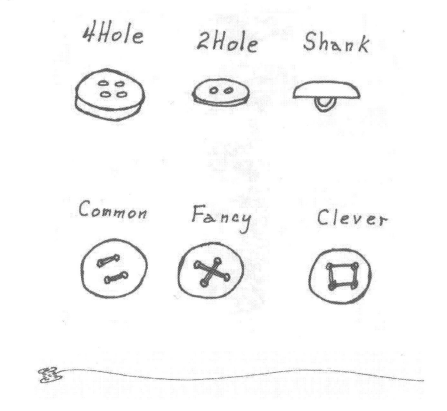

Photo 13-4

13-3) Tendency…Even though I convinced you to sew buttons using your sewing machine, I must admit there are buttons with a shank that must be sewed by hand.

The Problem…. There is always a catch.

To Clarify……..Here is where a sewing teacher can be a huge help. I always sit beside my students as I demonstrate the techniques of: threading the needle; sewing the button on in the correct spot; and this is my favorite, The Ledged of the Disappearing Thread. (See Tendency 4-4, pages 33-34) The needle will be pushed between the fashion fabric and the lining or facing. Suggested design detail: Try covering a button with your fashion fabric. It gives your garment a real professional look.

13-4) Tendency…After a pillow is stuffed; I have seen students attempt to sew the pillow opening closed by using the sewing machine.

The Problem….I say attempt because, the stuffing gives the pillow bulk and this makes it awkward and stiff. It would take a very strong vice to flatten the pillow enough to run it under the foot in order to make a decent seam or the pillow form is too small for the pillow cover you just sewed making it baggy. But if you want the baggy look, go for it.

To Clarify……..There are two ways to finish pillows and cushions. One way is to sew a zipper first (this will be at the bottom of the pillow) then sew the remaining three sides together. Be sure to unzip the zipper enough to pull the fabric through before you sew the remaining three sides. Next turn the pillow right side out through the opened zipper. Stuff the pillow form making sure it fits snuggly in all four corners. Zip it closed - you are done. However, sewing a pillow zipper is probably better done after you have developed more sewing skills. The second way to finish a pillow is to sew the opening closed by hand. Now don't get into a twit. Actually finishing a pillow in this fashion will allow you the freedom to carry on a conversation in class while hand sewing the final bottom edge. Pretty soon you will be finished and everyone can admire your handy work. To begin: sew (right sides together) about two inches back from the corner on the bottom edge. Note: Because you may have a printed fabric design that needs to be presented right side up such as trees or horses *take a moment* to be sure you are starting at the bottom of the design. Back stitch about 4 stitches. Stitch continuously around the remaining three sides. To avoid the pointy corners one sees in some finished pillows, reduce the stitch length close to 0 and take a few stitches at an angle across each corner. Lastly about two inches in from the last corner stop: back stitch. This will keep the stitches from coming undone as you stuff it. A sewing buddy will come in handy at this point. One stuffs the other maneuvers the fabric "sack". To close up the opening: turn in the SA and use a whipstitch at the edge knotting the thread every four inches or so. This makes the seam stronger. (Photo 13-4) The pillow form inside creates a thick edge while pinning it closed, therefore I recommend holding it by using the *quilters long pins with the flat flower head*. See arrow. This will help you while hand sewing: giving you the confidence that the opening will not gape open.

A sewing get together!

 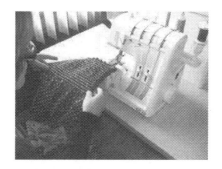

Sew many different projects!

 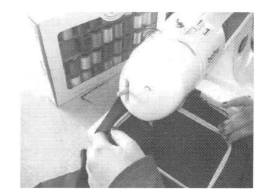

Sew many different machines!

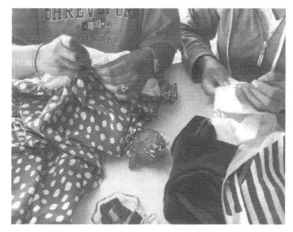 

Sew much fun!

Section V

Sewing Techniques

*The **Magic** is beginning and the **Mystery** is fading*

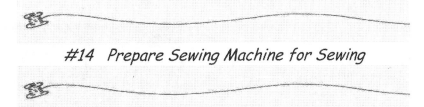

#14 Prepare Sewing Machine for Sewing

Drawing 14-1

Drawing 14-2

Photo 14-2

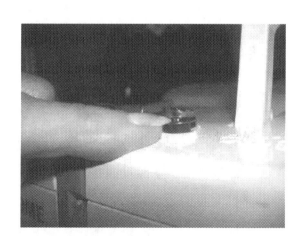

14-1) Tendency…Too often I see students placing the bobbin into the bobbin case with a thread wrapped around the edge of the bobbin. (Drawing 14-1) B A D ! **Really** B A D !

The Problem……It may not show up right away, but a thread jamb is only a matter of time.

To Clarify……...There is no room for this rouge thread inside the bobbin case. If there is, you may be using the wrong bobbin. Your machine will run more efficiently using the correct bobbin. So don't even take a chance, it is not worth it. I have my students prepare the bobbin for winding by placing the thread through the tension disc then slipping it through a small hole in the side of the bobbin <u>from the inside out</u>. Place the bobbin on the winder post firmly holding a 3" thread tail above the bobbin. The next details are most important for a solid wind in the bobbin. #1 you need to <u>hold the thread tail solidly in your fingers of your left hand</u>. Relax the thread a bit, not your grip. In the past sewers would pull up on the thread tail so hard it was like they could pick up the machine with the thread. Such power! #2 start filling the bobbin. The thread tail will coil up in your fingers. [If you should let go of the thread tail, it will wrap around the bobbins edge. If you do not catch it in time, the thread tail will get covered up in the winding process, making it impossible to pull it out. Unfortunately you will have to empty the entire bobbin: toss this thread.] #3 while still holding the thread tail, continue winding and watch the thread go up and down inside the bobbin as it fills. #4 after the thread goes up and down three or four times, take your foot <u>off</u> the foot peddle. #5 stretch out the thread and cut it (preferably with *small thread scissors*), right next to the bobbin leaving NO thread tail. #6 continue winding using a <u>steady even speed</u> with the foot peddle. Most machines will stop winding or slow down when the bobbin is full. #7 cut the thread and remove the bobbin from the spindle with a straight up motion. This will protect the plastic bobbins from getting cracks on the inside. Before placing the bobbin into its bobbin case, *take a moment* to make sure there is no thread wrapped around the edge of the bobbin. If you need more bobbins, take one to the store and purchase the <u>exact duplicate</u>. (I place the bobbin in an envelope and seal it, that way I will not loose it in my purse.) A word of caution: you do not need bunches of bobbins already filled because you will not remember how old the thread is and old thread will break and split and raise havoc with your machine. Wow! That was long winded. Following these instructions will reward you with a better sewing experience.

14-2) Tendency…Have you ever seen a bobbin look like this? (Drawing 14-2)

The Problem….Where do I begin? The wind is sloppy, lumpy, and loose on the bobbin post. If you get any seam at all it will be so bad it will not hold the fabric pieces together. Now you have to pull the thread off and start over. Operator error is usually the problem.

To Clarify……...Chances are the thread did not make it securely into the bobbin winding tension disk. (Photo 14-2 My fingernail has lifted the tension disk.) Operator error in this situation is speed. You are going to fast to realize the thread didn't get into the bobbin winding tension disk properly. SLOW DOWN just a bit. If you are still having problems try wrapping the thread one and a half times in the tension disk making sure it is completely inside. Another way to change the tension would be to loosen or tighten the screw, on top of the bobbin winding tension disk. Use your larger screwdriver. Turn the screw driver only slightly, a little turn goes a long way.

Photo 14-3

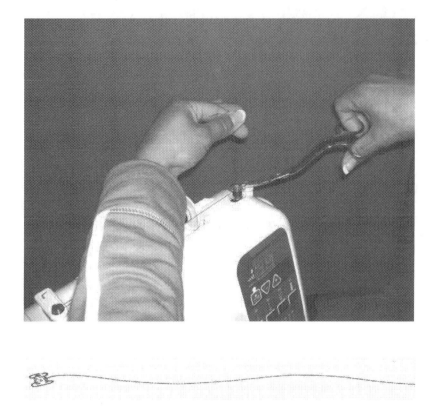

Photo 14-4

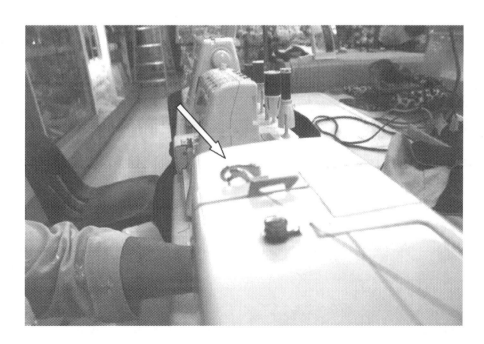

14-3) Tendency…Years ago we were taught to hold the thread up firmly as we wound the bobbin. Eventually the thread would break off. Of course we used <u>metal bobbins</u> which aided the <u>cotton thread</u> to snap off almost instantly.

The Problem….Today we use mostly plastic bobbins requiring a much longer time for the thread to snap off. To add to this predicament many of the threads today are made of polyester and have a stronger breaking point. I am convinced that we hold the thread too tight and can cause the bobbin winding spindle to drag. No wonder we get a bad wind.

To Clarify……..This is a repeat: but I am coming at it from a different perspective. To wind the bobbin, hold the thread tightly in your fingers of your <u>left</u> hand; now relax the thread but not your grip on the thread. In the <u>right</u> hand have the scissors or thread snips at the ready. Wind the bobbin so the thread covers the bobbins' post about three or four layers. Allow the thread to coil in your fingers, don't let go allowing the thread to get closer to the bobbin? <u>Stop the machine</u>, pull the thread straight up (left hand) and cut it right at the quick just outside the bobbin. (In Photo 14-4, my student used the embroidery thread scissors.) You do not want to leave any thread tail above the bobbin. Continue winding the bobbin. Be sure to keep your foot peddle at a constant speed. One time a student complained about the front of her bobbin blowing off as she was filling it. (Some Viking machines wind the bobbin in front.) What she was doing was winding clear thread (plastic) at a break-neck speed. The clear thread heated up and expanded. It was amazing she didn't get hurt. **SLOW DOWN**.

14-4) Tendency…"Where is your *take-up lever*?"

The Problem …..This one causes more trouble with manual machines than any other problem. The take-up lever <u>must</u> be at its highest position when you start and stop a seam. "<u>Please</u> make a note of it!" If the take-up lever is not at its highest position when you start sewing, more then likely you will loose the thread out of the needle. After a while you will discover the needle has been piercing the fabric but not making a seam. At the other end of your seam, if the take-up lever is not in the highest position, one or three things will happen:1) the fabric will not come out from under the foot because the needle is still in the fabric; 2) the needle may be out of the fabric but the fabric will not budge because the machine is still trying to make a stitch; or 3) if you are successful to pull the fabric towards the back and the take-up lever is still inside the slot , you now have three threads instead of two. (See Photo 15-9, page 131-132)

To Clarify………I can't tell you how many times students have expressed wonderment when this happens. I simply ask them, **"Where is your take-up lever?"** (Photo 14-4) A quick look will help identify the problem. To help my students understand how to correct the problem, I place my hand in front of the needle and instruct them to grasp the hand wheel and turn it forward like a Waterfall. I do this to force my students to look at the take-up lever instead of the needle. If the student looks at the needle they will raise it to its highest point, but the take-up lever is still down inside the slot. When the take-up lever is at its highest position, you can remove the fabric effortlessly. Keep practicing; you will get the hang of it, soon. Remember, Waterfall! Waterfall!

Drawing 14-5

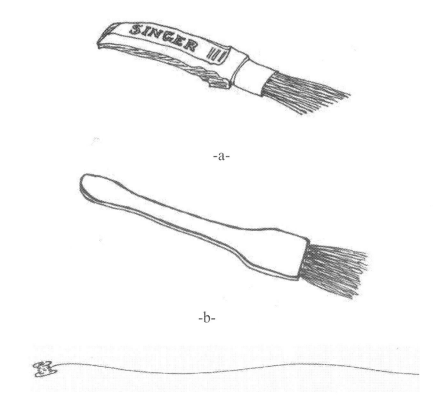

-a-

-b-

Photo 14-5

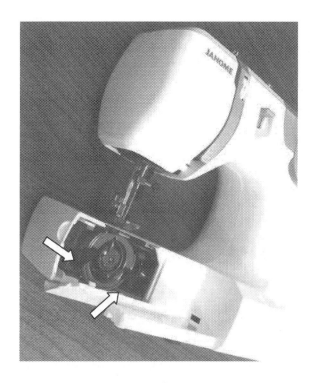

14-5) Tendency… Have you ever hear your machine getting louder and louder? May even start to smell a bit? Also, if you have been sewing nonstop, like so many of us, a potential thread jamb (lock) could develop.

The Problem…. If you are using a mechanical sewing machine it is probably dry. Dry or not, lint can build up in the bobbin case area and all around the feed teeth. All fabrics produce lint. The major contributors are flannel and the ever popular fleece. Lint build-up goes triple for the serging machine looper area because of the blade cutting off the excess fabric SA.

To Clarify………Front bobbin loading machines need oil on the inside of the circle thingy. (Drawing 16-2, page 141-142) Just one drop will do nicely. You can oil your machines with the help of your manual. If you do not have your manual your teacher can help. Use *SEWING MACHINE OIL*, <u>ONLY</u>! Computerized sewing machines will require a service technician to oil your machine. Depending on how often you use either machine you should take them to the sewing machine technician annually or every two year. If you have not used your sewing machine for more than two years, definitely take it to the service technician before sewing with it. Regular maintenance is a must if you want your machine to give you full service. Clean the entire area before oiling. Here are the steps to prepare the front loading bobbin case area for cleaning and oiling: 1) remove the bobbin and its case. 2) Carefully lay the machine on its back. If your foot lever is directly behind the needle shaft, ease it down before you lay the machine on its back. Removing the circle thingy will be much easier. 3) Release the two black levers in an outward motion. Note the two arrows. (Photo 14-5) Place both forefingers on the inside of the circle thingy. Use an upward movement to lift the circle thingy straight up. It will lift out without any trouble. In-other-words you do not have to force it. The last piece to remove is the hook. 4) Simply hold on to the center post and lift upwards. 5) Now you can get in there and really clean. Be sure to clean all the parts because lint is every where. When you purchase a machine it comes with several tools. One of which is a lint brush. Many sewing and serging manufacturers include a puny brush with their machines. They work but because the brush is so small you wind up working twice as hard. If yours is the puny type I encourage you to buy the *Singer lint brush*. (Drawing 14-5a) The *Singer brush* is truly an efficient tool due to the long full bristles cut at an angle. It really gets into the cracks and crevasses while lifting out the lint and rendering the area clean. Also the fabulous curved handle with a soft surface feels comfortable in the hand. My serger came with this wonderful brush. (Drawing 14-5b) For sergers, check the upper looper shaft often. Lint stacks up there as well. I really get in there and clean like mad. After brushing out the lint take a thin scrap of cloth and clean the area again. When your lint brush gets to looking dirty (oil and lint collecting on the bristles) simply wash it with soapy water; rinse well with cool water and dry completely. Good, now the brush is ready for the next cleaning. Remember, one drop of oil is sufficient for both sewing and serging machines. *Canned Air* helps to blow out the lint. If you have a vacuum, I recommend getting the *Mini Attachment Kit*, it sucks the lint out. It works perfectly! For further information, check the Threads Magazine article; <u>Keep your machine in tip top shape</u>, May 2007, number 130, pages 29 – 31. Remember: machines can freeze up when not used for more then 2 years.

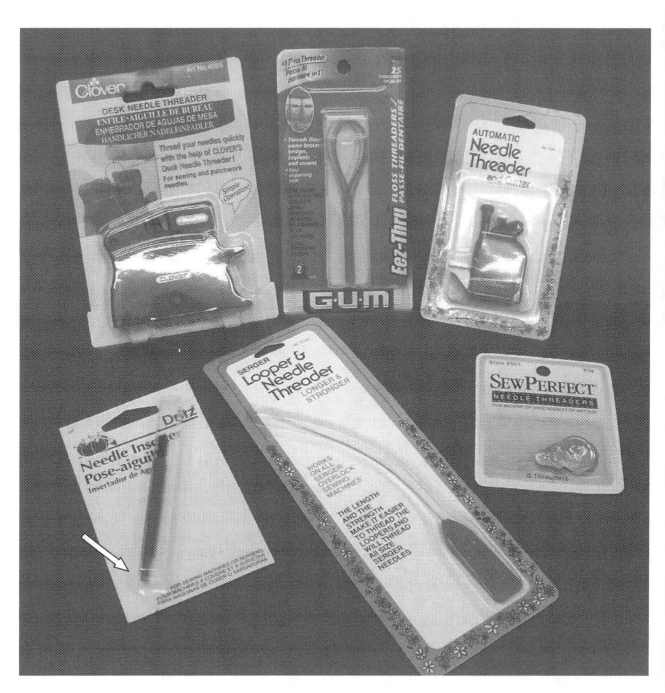

Need a needle threader? There are so many to choose from. Even a Floss threader will do nicely!
Try the Sewing machine Needle Inserter, sure makes changing the needle less tedious. Arrow
shows location of hole where you put the sewing machine needle.
Excellent instructions come with the tool.

#15 A Few Sewing Techniques

Photo 15-1

Photo 15-2

-a-

-b-

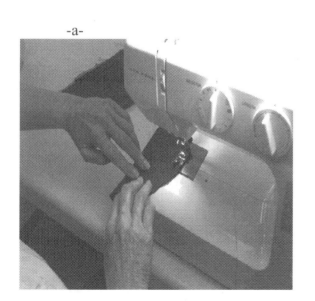
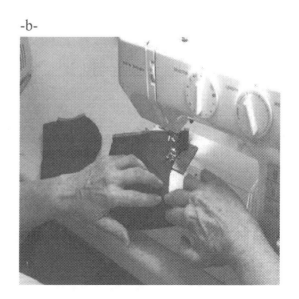

15-1) Tendency…I continually see students with flat heavy hands on the machine while sewing: putting too much pressure on the fabric as it travels under the foot.

The Problem …..This causes the fabric to stretch and makes the machine work too hard! Another problem occurs when lifting one hand while the machine is running: this gets real interesting. Beginners tend to get off tract. Sewing dangerously close to the cut edge is crucial when the fabric frays easily. Guiding the fabric with the <u>right</u> hand makes the SA get wider. On the other hand (no pun intended), guiding the fabric with your <u>left</u> hand makes the SA get narrower. The result is a wobbly seam. Fabric that frays can disintegrate and develop gaps in the seam making the finished garment terribly unsightly and uncomfortable. This will need to be mended provided there is any fabric left to close up the seam. I can just hear Winnie the Pooh say: "Oh, Bother".

To Clarify……….Not to worry! Believe it or not, a *Midas touch* is all you need for <u>most</u> sewing. Generally, a SA (seam allowances) is sewed at 5/8" from the cut edge of the fabric. Curve your fingers of both hands and place them on the fabric at the front of the machine. (Photo15-1) Now, let the machine pull your hands and the fabric to the foot, together. Don't go too fast. Of course if you have long fingernails my method will be more difficult. However, I see my students sewing a much straighter seam when they exert the same slight pressure with the fingertips of both hands. Curving your finders helps to:

a.   Ease finger fatigue, because you are using less pressure on the fabric as you sew;

b.   Keeps you from sewing your fingers (providing you place all fingers on the fabric);

c.   Sew a nice straight line;

d.   Sew curves more accurately, (See Tendency below);

e.   Keeps you from leaning the heels of your hands on the machine.

15-2) Tendency…"I can "never" sew in a curve so don't make me!"

The Problem ……One of the hardest sewing skills on the sewing machine (for beginners) is to learn how to sew in a curve. "Never say never", is my missions in life. We women tend to work to hard at our tasks. Instead we simply figure out another way of solving the problem.

To Clarify……… Guess what? You can do it! All you need to do is to use the *Midas touch* with your fingertips. Move the fabric (inside curve or outside curve) <u>after</u> the machine starts, not before. To accomplish this, once the machine is engaged, move the fabric towards the right (Photo 15-2a) for an outside curve; and to the left (Photo 15-2b) for an inside curve. You know, it's like walking: right foot forward and left arm forward: etcetera. To the right of the foot are marks indicating different SA's. When sewing curved seams, I watch the appropriate SA indicator to the right of the needle. This helps me sew a smoother curved seam. Practice this method and you will see it really works. Slow down. In contrast, don't move at a snails pace either. Practice will give you confidence. In the photo my wrists are at an awful angle because I needed to get my body and shoulders out of the cameras way. Having a sense of humor helps make your time sewing more pleasant and definitely productive. How about that: you do not have to wait to reach the advanced stage in your sewing carrier to sew curves. Nice!

Drawing 15-3

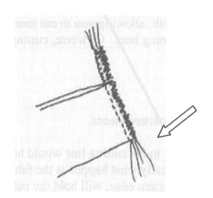

Photo 15-4

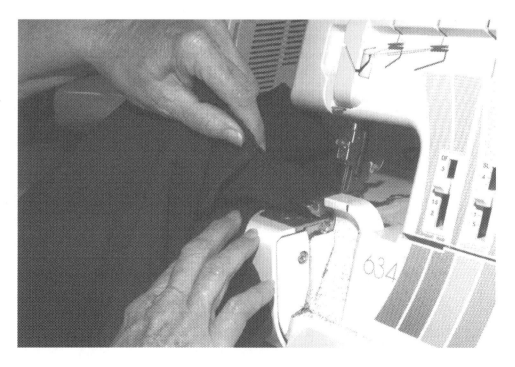

15-3) Tendency…"Oh Dear, my serged seam has come undone!" Now what do I do?

The Problem….. When you are using a regular sewing machine you can cut the thread right at the end of the seam provided you take just a few, two or three, stitches in reverse. However, when you are using a serging machine it is not wise to cut the thread at the end of the seam. "Gee Whiz", if you cut the thread chain close to the end of the serged seam, the threads will separate easily and the seam will come undone. (See arrow Drawing 15-3) Remember, <u>the serger does not sew in reverse</u>.

To Clarify……… At the end of each seam, it is a good idea to continue pressing your foot on the peddle so you can make a four inch thread chain. <u>Gently</u> pull your fabric towards the back while serging the thread chain. Stop serging, then cut the thread chain about two inches from the end of the seam. This allows you to have a sufficient amount of thread chain to start the next seam. The *serger work book* will demonstrate a handy way to <u>secure</u> the thread chain at the beginning and end of each seam. Once this is done, you can cut the thread close to the fabric. Now that you have worked a little bit with your serger, *take a class*, the teacher should be able to help you understand how to secure the seams and many other techniques. When you purchase your Serger at a reputable dealer they will have available to purchase a comprehensive *Workbook* written special for your machine. I recommend buying the book, it will help you ten fold. This tendency is dedicated to my friend Danielle. I hope it will encourage her to dust off her serger (5 year ownership: 0 use) and get it serviced and start enjoying the benefits of sewing with her serger.

15-4) Tendency…"What is this? Do I have to rip out?"

The Problem ….. Some times we work so fast we create: puckers; sew other parts of the fabric into the SA (seam allowance) or worse yet the undetected SA folds under the foot getting caught in the seam. RRRRRipping time! Current phrase is "unsewing". Some fabrics are so delicate that this will leave holes in it. Not good. And, serged seams are extremely tedious when you have to rip out.

To Clarify……….Smooth and flat is what you will hear me say many times in class. This goes double when you are feeding mounds of fabric through the machine. Generally we sew with the SA to the right of the needle because pushing mounds of fabric between the needle unit and the motor housing can get mighty tight. The fabric must be smooth and flat on both sides of the foot. Before you resume sewing, check under the fabric to make sure there is no extra fabric that you do not want to sew. (Photo15-4) Look under the fabric often as you sew. Now you know the area where the seam is to be sewed is flat and other parts of the garment have not slipped under the foot. After a while your fingers will be able to tell if there is a piece of fabric under the foot that is not supposed to be there. But do not rest on your laurels, check often! Recently I completed a lushes taffeta Opera Coat. I had to be continuously aware of the bundles of fabric running under the foot. Everyone said it was gorgeous and was bought for a hansom price at a local auction.

Photo 15-5

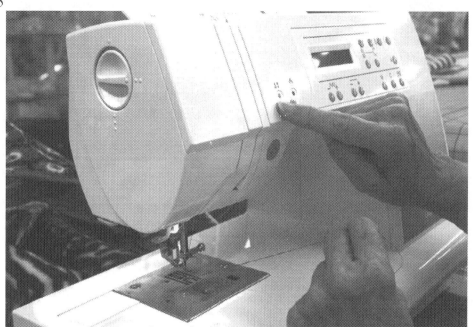

Drawing 15-6

GAP IN SEAM

OOPS!

15-5) Tendency…Now that the bobbin is in and the machine is threaded, what is next?

The Problem ….The sewing machine is threaded and there is no fabric under the foot: the needle is up but the take-up-lever is not all the way up. Now is NOT a good time to touch the needle up/down icon (see page 141-142) or turn the hand wheel (Waterfall) or step on the foot-peddle, Oops! Simply put, you will be setting up your machine for a thread lock (jam).

To Clarify……..<u>Hold the top thread out in front</u> while turning the hand wheel or tapping the needle up-down button. (Photo 15-5) Gently pull the thread forward as and turn the hand wheel one full revolution. Gently I said; you do not want to have gobs of thread in your hand. Stop when the take-up lever is at its highest point. (See the threads where they interlock? You just made a stitch in air.) Holding the thread in front will keep you from getting a thread lock (jam). [I removed the foot, for this photo, in order for you to see the needle down in the machine as I hold the thread.]

15-6) Tendency…If a seam is not sewed all the way to the end, you may be creating a gap.

The Problem …..This is rather important when a second seam will be sewn across this unsown section. (Drawing 15-6)

To Clarify……..For most sewing machines, there are three sets of feed teeth: on either side of the needle plate hole as well as behind the needle plate whole. To begin a seam, place the fabric completely under the foot so the back feed teeth are covered. Ease down on the foot peddle a few stitches in reverse to the end of the fabric but do not sew in air. Do this slowly! If you do not sew a couple of stitches in reverse, the seam can come undone. It is <u>not</u> necessary to sew a whole bunch of stitches in reverse, a couple is plenty. You only want to keep the stitching from coming undone. Ripping out so many reverse stitches can be tedious and time consuming. Be sure to hold the thread tails and pull gently away from the needle as you start sewing forward to eliminate that nasty bunched up fabric at the start of your seam. At the end of your seam you do not want to sew off the fabric either, beyond the fabric, **sew slowly**. You could be setting up still another thread jamb. Instead, stop one stitch shy of the end of the fabric and take a couple of stitches in reverse. Piling up stitches is not necessary, save this for mending. Make sure the take-up lever is at its highest point, lift the foot firmly, grab the fabric as close to the end of the seam as possible pulling your fabric towards the back left corner. (See Tendency 2-11, page 17) Cut the thread at the end of the seam. Your seam is complete: now on to the next.

Drawing 15-7

Photo 15-8

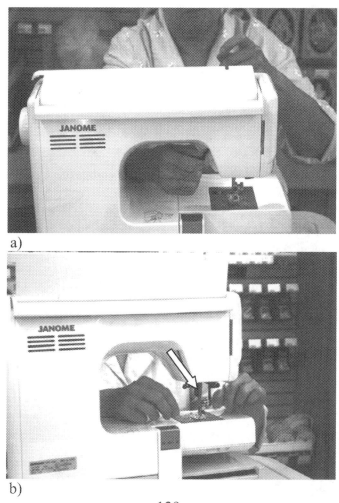

a)

b)

15-7) Tendency…"I am confused, where does the thread go?"

The Problem……Each machine uses slightly different thread guides. If you have your *machine manual*, follow the drawings: some times they can be difficult to understand. Should you miss thread, the machine may not sew a decent seam. This is called "operator error". If not threaded correctly the *serging machines* will not create a seam at all. You will have four threads unattached, waving in the breeze.

To Clarify……….The threads are placed in several thread guides as well as 2 vertical slots. I highly recommend taking a *sewing class* from your local *sewing teacher*. (Drawing 15-7) She will be able to help you find the correct thread guides. Also the teacher can show you how to thread the eye of the needle correctly. Now I know that last statement sounds a little strange but when the thread gets wrapped around the needle it can cause a multitude of problems. The newer sewing machines have a clever needle threading devise; however this will take much practice to get it down. Your teacher can be a big help. My first dozen or so attempts to use the needle threader turned out disastrous. Sometimes I would be successful but most of the time I would miss. I did not understand the workings until I took a magnifying glass and examined it closely. Once I understood the system, the needle threader became a great time saver; not to mention saving my eye sight. The hook that grabs the thread is very tiny and can bend or break easily. The sewing machine technician dreads replacing the hook. My advice is to not slam down the needle threading lever. Instead, ease it down. And practice many times. You'll get the hang of it.

15-8) Tendency…"Something is wrong with my machine, the seam doesn't look right. Do I change the top tension dial?"

The Problem …… If you threaded the machine with the foot in the down position, the thread will NOT be in the tension disc. I am surprised when my students get a seam at all. Rats, now you must rip out what stitch you did get and rethread your sewing machine, again.

To Clarify……….Changing the top tension is not necessarily what is needed! In most cases the tension dial is the last thing to change. In the beginning, most people go to the top tension dial first. To avoid having to rethread or, dare I say, prevent a potential thread lock, take a *moment* to check the foot lever to see if it is in the up or down position before threading your machine. There is that *moment* again! If it is in the down position: simply raise the lever to lift the foot, no not the one you stand on, then resume threading your machine. (Photo 15-8 a, b) Note: Some of the upper end sewing and embroidery machines have a knee lever to elevate the foot, freeing your hand to guide the fabric more efficiently. Nice!

Photo 15-9

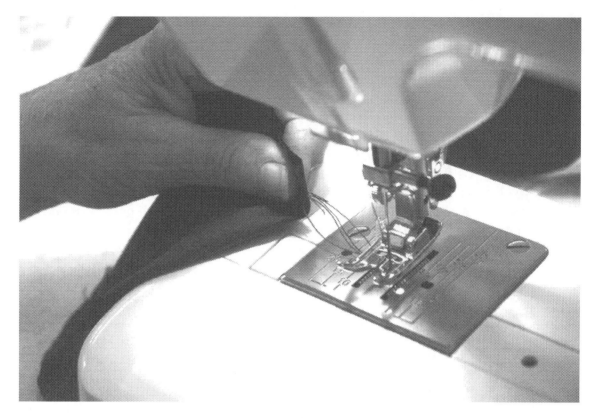

Actually I count 4 threads. I wonder where the 4th thread came from. Oh Dear! Another mystery!

15-9) Tendency…"How come I have three threads coming out of the bobbin area?"

The Problem ……Well, your needle is out of the fabric and it is really hard to pull the fabric towards the back of the machine: plus now you have <u>three</u> threads. (Photo 15-9) "**Three threads?** I thought there were only supposed to be two threads."

To Clarify……… If the take-up lever is <u>not</u> at its highest position, the machine is still trying to complete a stitch. What you see is the needle thread doubled over in the middle of making a stitch, hence, the three threads. Simple solution! I tell my students to look at the <u>take-up lever</u> **before** raising the foot. On most new machines the take-up lever stops at its highest position all on its own, nice! But if it does not, take a moment and turn the hand wheel (Waterfall, Waterfall) until you see the take-up lever at its highest position. Use the needle up-down button or the needle icon/button on the screen, if you have these features. (See page 141-142) Now raise the foot and firmly but gently pull the fabric towards the back left corner of the machine. This way your <u>two threads</u> will stay under the foot and to the back freeing you from having to realign them later. The photo actually shows four threads. Don't have a clue where the fourth thread came from: what? We have another **mystery?** You might check the bobbin case area carefully for a rogue thread that may have become lodged in the works. Just follow the above direction and your sewing projects will come out OKAY!

Photos 15-10 a-f

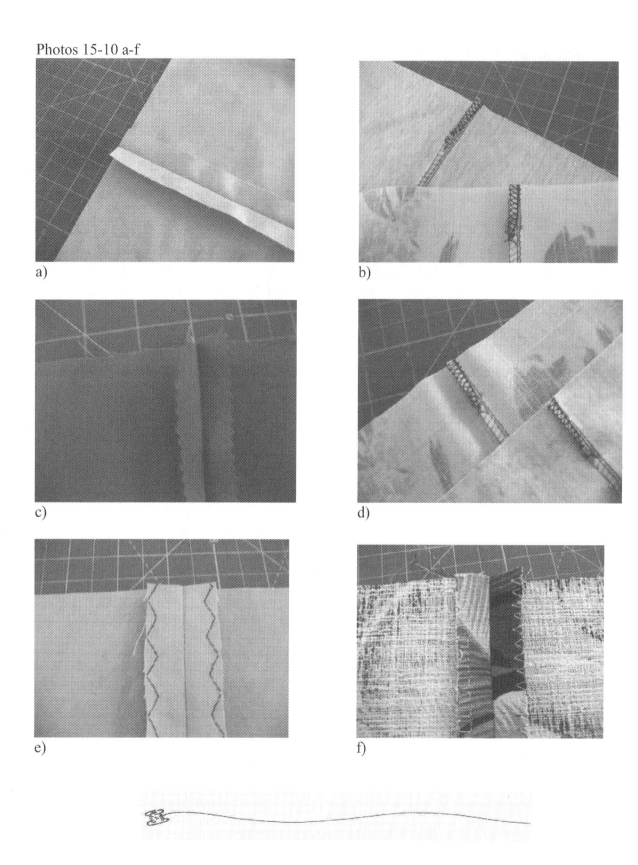

a)

b)

c)

d)

e)

f)

15-10) Tendency...So many edge finishes, which one do I use?

The Problem......Some fabrics are OKAY when left unfinished. But others need more care to avoid curling up or fraying; also some seams are in stress areas and need to be *stabilized*.

To Clarify..........The following is a quick reference suggesting the different edge finishes and the proper fabric for each finish: from the basic to the more labor intensive. Pressing SA open is understood, no pressing will be noted.

Seam type	Edge finish required	Fabric weave and weight
a) regular seam - Sew M* pressed open		tight woven light, medium
b) serged seam - Serg M*1 pressed to one side		woven & knit light, medium
c) regular seam – Sew M pinked edges		woven light, medium
d) regular seam - Sew M zig-zag stitch		woven light, medium
e) regular seam - Sew M multi zig-zag stitch		woven medium, heavy
f) regular seam - Sew M overcast stitch		woven light, medium, heavy

* Sew M means Sewing Machine
*1 Ser M means Serging Mahcine

Photos 15-10 g-j

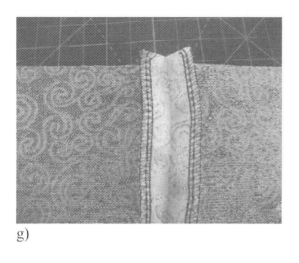
g)

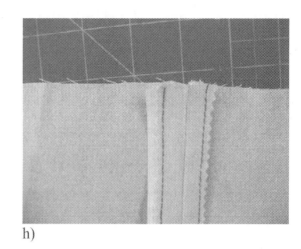
h)

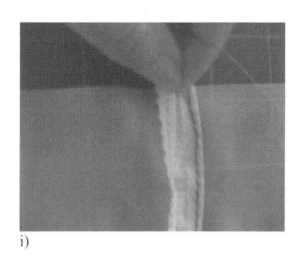
i)

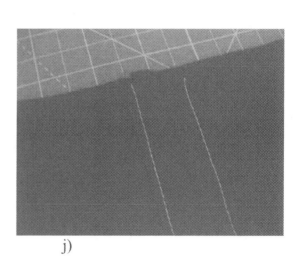
j)

Tendency 15-10 (continued)

Seam type	Edge finish required	Fabric weave and weight
g) regular seam - Ser M not part of seam		woven light, medium, heavy
h) regular seam – Sew M pinked and straight stitched		woven medium, heavy
i) regular seam – Sew M pinked, fold and straight stitched		woven light
j) regular seam – Sew M triple seam stabilizing stress area		woven light, medium, heavy

Photos 15-10 k-p

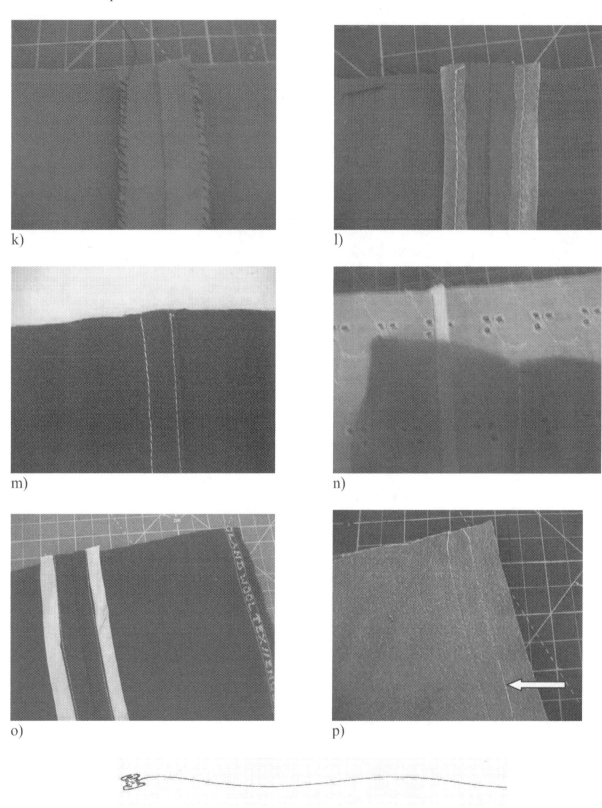

k)

l)

m)

n)

o)

p)

Tendency 15-10 (continued)

When you reach intermediate level, try the following. Ask your teacher for assistance:

Seam type	Edge finish required	Fabric weave and weight
k) regular seam – Sew M hand whip stitch		woven light
l) regular seam – Sew M net bound		velvet, chiffon, and loose weave
m) Flat-felled Seam – Sew M sew twice		denim, corduroy, medium twill
n) French Seam – Sew M sew twice		woven sheers
o) Hong Kong Finish – Sew M sew twice each edge		woven heavy, unlined jackets
p) Vogue Stretch Stitch –Sew M no need for edge finish set controls: 1 length & 1 width (zig-zag)		knit suede cloth does not fry use press cloth with iron

Note: In photo p) there are 2 seams, the right seam has skipped stitches.(See arrow) The left seam has been corrected by using a *Stretch Stitch Needle*. Because the eye is a little higher, this needle can correct some of your sewing machines problems: automatically, nice.

Special note: Tassle Orozco is my sewing machine specialist and personal friend. He gave me
another wonderful reason for turning the light off when away from the machine. The
heat from the light bulb dries up the sewing machine oil. My recommendation
for turning the light bulb off is to keep from accidentally tapping
the foot peddle as you return to the machine
creating a thread jam.

#16 A Few Causes for Thread Jam's

16-1   Birds nest thread jam

16-2   This one can damage your machine

16-3   Did not bring up the bobbin thread through the needle

16-4   Forget to lower the foot down before sewing a seam

Drawing 16-1

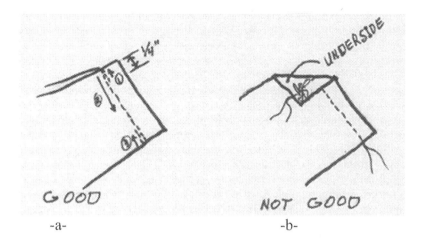

GOOD

-a-

UNDERSIDE

NOT GOOD

-b-

Drawings 16-2

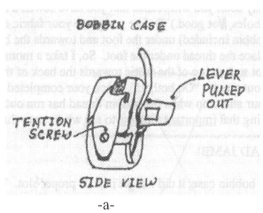

BOBBIN CASE

LEVER
PULLED
OUT

TENTION
SCREW

SIDE VIEW

-a-

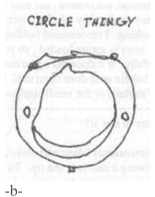

CIRCLE THINGY

-b-

16-1) Tendency...T H R E A D   J A M, or birds nest.

The Problem .....What a nasty mess! More ripping out! There are so many ways to tangle the sewing thread. Some times you can not see the tangled thread because it is on the underside of the seam. The most common way to cause a thread jam is to start sewing right at the edge of the fabric causing the thread to get tangled up in several thread loops. Not a pretty picture, plus if you start cutting the loops the seam may come undone.

To Clarify..........I have mentioned this procedure before and it does not hurt to repeat it again. My recommendation is to starting sewing about ¼" from the edge of the fabric, take two or three stitches in reverse, then sew forward. (Drawing 16-1a) This does two things.1) the feed dogs (teeth) in the center have a good hold on the fabric layers helping them move smoothly; and 2) the fabric will not bunch up at the beginning of the seam. (Drawing 16-1b) You will labor in vain if you try to press the bunched up seam open. Take a *moment* to make sure the take-up lever is at its highest position. Now you are absolutely ready to start your seam. The drawing 16-1a shows reverse stitches side by side. Actually, your machine will sew on tip of the these stitches. I offer this category to help you understand a simple rule. You can solve just about any Thread Jam if you know what you have done to get into that predicament. Setting up good habits will create an environment of happy and productive hours of sewing. Note: The newer more expensive sewing machines have pretty much corrected this obstacle. F a n t a s t i c!

16-2) Tendency...Another THREAD JAM, only worse, this one can damage your machine.

The Problem .... Yes, this is a serious problem. For the front loading machines the bobbin case must find its way into its proper slot. If you should see the bar (part sticking up in Drawing 16-2 a) any where else but pointing up you could have a serious problem. To install the front loading bobbin case you could just shove it into the bobbin case area. Over time this will damage the mechanism inside the bobbin case, and may not catch causing it to jam inside the *circle thingy*. (Drawings16-2b) See answer 14-5, page 120. Too many times I have had to say a little prayer to help me free up my students trapped bobbin case without breaking something. *Scary!*

To Clarify..........I recommend holding the lever out until the bobbin and bobbin case nestles completely in the *circle thingy* with the bar pointing upwards. On the bobbin case, there is a spring loaded lever. You need to hold this lever out securely until the bobbin case is completely installed. Some Viking sewing machines have two bars in the bobbin case. Squeeze these bars together using your thumb and forefinger until the bobbin case is completely installed. Next, release the bars (Viking) or lever (standard bobbin case) and jiggle the bobbin case forcefully with my fingers. If it does not fall out: IT'S IN. HALLELUIAH! At this point I encourage my students to leave the bobbin case hatch open until they bring up the bobbin thread using the hand wheel (Waterfall, Waterfall) or the needle up/down button or the tough screen icon. After you pull the bobbin thread up, (See Tendency 16-3 page 143-144) close the bobbin case hatch. I like to install the bobbin case first then thread the sewing machine. This is my routine, it works for me and I am sticking to it! Now I am ready to sew. Practice this and it will take no time at all to get your machine ready for action.

Photo 16-3

I just noticed the top thread did not get into the last guide (see arrow). Oops!
May not hurt but you never know, so make sure you get the thread in all the thread guides.

Photo 16-4

16-3)Tendency…"What! Another Thread Jam?"

The Problem…… And right at the beginning of your seam, rats! You probably did not bring up the bobbin thread. Having to pull out the bobbin case and clean out the tangled thread and rethread everything before you sew a seam is time consuming and discouraging.

The Answer…… After you put the bobbin in the machine, you need to bring it up through the needle plate. Use your left hand to hold the needle thread between the needle and you. Next, turn the hand wheel, (remember Waterfall) and at the same time slowly pulling the needle thread towards you. Then something magical happens. The bobbin thread is captured and brought up via the needle and through the needle plate. How about that! It worked! No more mystery! (Photo 16-3) Next grab the loop (bobbin thread) and pull until you see the end of the thread coming up through the needle plate. With one motion, I use the *seam gauge* to guide the two threads to there proper spot under and behind the foot. I hope you are getting the idea that thread jams are mostly *operator error*. Note: On manual sewing machines the needle may get stuck, I mean *really stuck*. When this happens I take an *old small wooden thread spool* and place it under the needle screw. Then with my left hand I hold the outer ring really steady (*Hand Wheel*) and forcefully turn, with my right hand, the inner wheel towards me. You may have to stand up to do this. However, if the needle is still jammed you will need to take the machine to your *sewing machine service center.*

16-4) Tendency…Here comes another THREAD JAM!

The Problem….. I find that my new students more often then not forget to lower the foot before sewing a seam. Sewing with really thick fabric may hide the fact that the foot is still up. Remember, when the foot is up there is no tension on the upper thread and can cause a thread jams.

To Clarify………There is always something to do before you can engage your sewing machine. Some feet are difficult to tell if they are in the down position. Therefore it is a good idea to reach for the foot lever before you start your machine. Make adjustments, if needed. After a while this will become second nature to you. But, don't rest on your laurels. It happened to me not too long ago. I had to take the fabric out, clean out the tangled threads in the fabric and bobbin case area and start all-over again. I could have spent that time sewing. Gee, if I had only checked the foot lever! The *Walking Foot,* because of its size, can fool even the more accomplished seamstresses. (Photo16-4) The Pffaf sewing machine has a permanently built-in walking foot unit located behind the foot: allowing the two fabrics to stay together instead of sliding and making the seams uneven. A very nice feature! As for fabrics: fleece, very popular today, is rather thick. The same goes for your quilting projects. Well, you might ask, how do I get these heavy fabrics under the foot? Remember the foot lever? Take the lever firmly in your hand and push upwards and hold it at its highest position. Now look at the foot to see how much elevation you gained. This takes same strength so be prepared. You should be able to get enough height to slide your fabric under the foot. Should the pile (the fuzzy part of the fleece) grab onto the feed teeth, I recommend pinning a piece of paper to the underside of the fabric then sliding the fleece fabric between the teeth and the foot. Once the fabric is in the correct spot for the seam, be sure to remove the pin and the paper. Did you lower the foot????????????

Buttons! Hems! Seams! So many repairs. Fixing one at a time is well within your capability!

#17 Life happens, mending must be done

17-1   Buttons fall off, safety pinning the area closed will not do!

17-2   Hems fall down, staples will not do!

17-3   Seams rip open, warning a garment with opened seams will not do!

17-4   It really helps to take sewing lessons!

Drawing 17-1

Photo 17-1 button foot

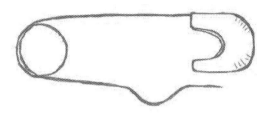

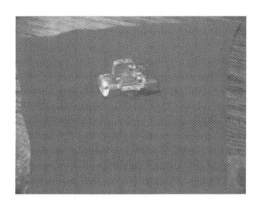

Photo 17-2a

Photo 17-2b

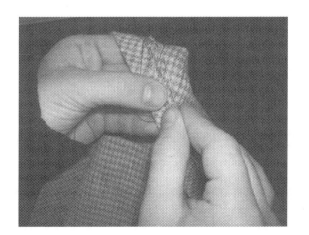

17-1) Tendency…Using a safety pin in the place of a button.

The Problem…..Chances are no one will ask you to sew on a button for them! However a safety pin will work in a pinch.

To Clarify……...If you can not find a safety pin shaped like the one in Drawing 17-1; go to a sewing class. There are 2 things to do when sewing on a button with your machine: dropping the feed teeth or snapping a plate over the feed teeth. 1) drop the feed dogs or snap the plate over them, 2) snap on the *button foot,* Photo 17-1, 4) 3) adjust the controls to a plain zig-zag stitch, set the width midway and you are ready to sew your button back on. To prepare the fabric: use a pin or a fabric marker to mark where you want to sew the button. Slide the garment under the foot first then ease the button under the foot. Make sure your fabric is not hanging over the edge of the table; gravity has a nasty way of pulling everything to the floor. Lower the foot carefully. Check the *swing* of the needle: I like to start with the left side of the zig-zag? Carefully lower the needle in the left hole in the button. Hopefully you will not crack the button and break the needle. **Be careful!** Now, raise the needle using the hand wheel (not backwards, please, like a Waterfall) and lower it into the right hole. If the needle is headed for the button surface, adjust the width regulator so the needle will not strike it. Try again lowering the needle. When the needle manages to fit into both holes it is time to sew. Using your foot: the one you stand on is now in order. Placing your Metatarsal arch way up on the foot peddle; sew no more then seven or nine stitches back and forth. Stop sewing when the needle is coming out of the right hole. Next you want to go from zig-zag to a straight stitch making sure the needle penetrates the center of the hole. Do this because you are going to sew 3 times in this hole to tie-off the stitches. Your button is on to stay. Some sewing machines will not let you sew in place. This will be different with each machine so test the width and/or needle position selectors: CAREFULLY! Your sewing teacher can be a big help provided she has experience on the different machines. I know it is confusing but with practice you will become competent very soon.

17-2) Tendency…Using double sided tape or, heaven for bid, staples are only a temporary fix for a fallen hem.

The Problem…..First thing when you wash the garment the tape will probably wash out. Or, even worse, staples will scratch your skin and could snag your pantyhose. Not a pretty picture.

To Clarify……...Carefully pin the fallen hem. With hand needle and thread sew the hem. Take care to catch only one thread of the skirt fabric then two or three threads on the inside top of the hem: continue sewing. (Photo 17-2a) There are three different machines that will produce a hem: your sewing machine; a serging machine and a blind hem machine. Some sergers have a cover hem capability. The blind hem machine, well that is all it does and handsomely too. Then there is your sewing machine. You can use a twin needle to produce the cover hem, nice on fleece fabric (Photo 17-2b). Or you can use the blind hem foot on woven fabric, a sewing teacher can help you understand how-to fold the fabric. Lastly your machine probably came with the rolled hem foot to sew what is commonly called shirt tail hem, nice for thin fabric. Again ask your teacher to demonstrate this technique. They all work exceedingly well. Now if you do not have the space or money to invest in three machines your regular sewing machine can get the job done. (Photo 17-2b shows a regular sewing machine using twin needles.)

Photo 17-3a

Photo 17-3b

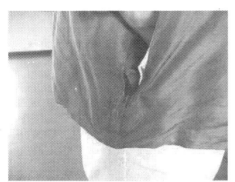

No need to toss the garment.

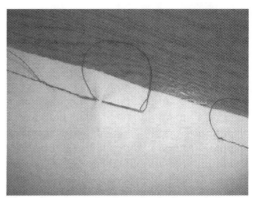

Sew the seam by hand - left to right

Photo 17-4

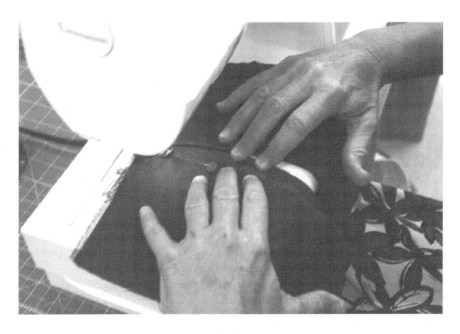

17-3) Tendency…A garment with ripped open seams (Photo 17-3a) is another clue that you do not have confidence in your ability to mend your garments.

The Problem…..The ripped seam could get considerably larger as you ware the garment. "Oh No"

To Clarify….…..See Tendency 15-1, page 123-124 for hand placement on the fabric as you sew the seam. Or when you are in a rush and your sewing machine is put away, take out your handy dandy sewing kit in the bottom of your purse and use a left to right back stitch. In Photo17-3b I used a white fabric with a black thread to indicate how the needle goes into the fabric at the seam line. This is only a temporary remedy until you can get to your trusty sewing machine. If you should be mending the spandex fabrics your seam may not hold for more then a one time ware because of the stretchiness. Using the hand held device to mend with is also only a quick fix, however, I do not recommend this tool. In a <u>real application</u> use thread that is a shade darker then the fashion fabric.

17-4) Tendency…I don't know how to repair a zipper, but it costs an arm and a leg to pay for this service.

The Problem…...If you do not learn how to use the different feet; your sewing hands; proper posture; the correct needles, and so on, then you will not realize how efficient the sewing machine and yourself can be. Not to mention all that money you wasted at the dry cleaners.

To Clarify….….. The other day I needed an apron and was able to whip it up in minutes. SIGN-UP FOR SEWING LESSONS! When special needs arrive, you will be prepared. Cultivating many sewing skills as a result of your sewing lessons renders you extremely creative and quick. In my classes I teach students to use both hands on the fabric as it travels to the needle/foot area. (Photo17-1, also see tendency 15-1, page 123-124) My method isn't the only way: but it does work. Each teacher will have her own way of sewing. Follow her style until you get comfortable; then develop your own style of sewing. I still practice several techniques I learned from my first tailoring teacher many years ago. You won't believe how self-fulfilling and fun sewing can be until you take sewing lessons in a class with other students at different skill levels. Some teachers will have a sewing machine you can use for a month to see if you really like to sew. If you find you do not like sewing, at least you haven't spent big money for a sewing machine. And you will have one sewing project to your credit, plus the skills to keep the mending pile down to a mild roar. **<u>"Just do it!"</u>** Note: Reread my message on page iii.

Remember when you used to say……..

Tendency…"I don't do: zippers; buttons; buttonholes; interfacings; darts (what ever they are); hand sewing; what are these things for? And the list goes on?

Solution…..SIGN-UP FOR A CLASS! Until you do, you won't believe how wonderful sewing can be! When you learn how to use your sewing machine, the different feet, proper posture, what to do with your hands, etcetera; your sewing experience will be a source of *pure pleasure*. One of my favorite phrases I use in class is "Put your foot down………not the one you stand on!"

WANT AD:

Beginning
Sewing Lessons
Mondays From 6pm to 9pm.
Bring your Sewing
or Serging Machine; a
pair of scissors; fresh thread;
and the desire to learn every-
thing about your machine.
Reserve your place in class.
Limit, 6 students.
XXX-XXX-XXXX

Section VI

Computerized Machines

Patterns

Now you know sewing does not have to be a **mystery!**

You want ME to buy a Computerized Sewing Machine?
No – No – No!

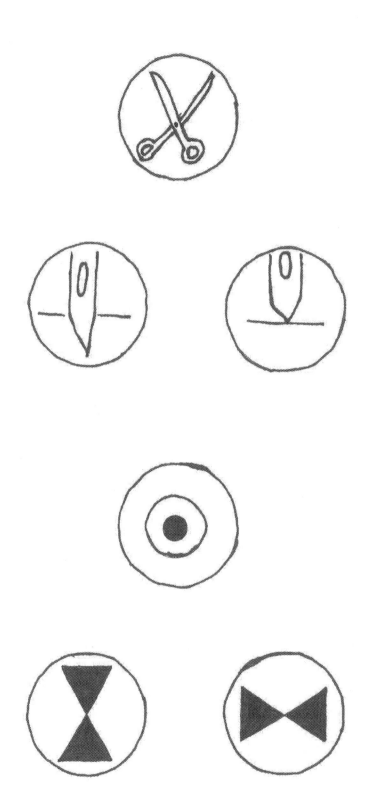

~~Four very nice features on the Computerized Sewing Machines~~

Scissors button or touch screen icon

The upper line sewing machines have a special button with a scissors icon on it. When you touch this button the sewing machine will cut the threads and raise the foot. WOW! Nice! Hugh! The *scissor icon* sometimes is placed on the *touch screen*. Check the manual for its location.

Needle up/down button or touch screen icon

Your sewing machine will not know you have finished your seam. Unfortunately, the needle could be in the down position making it impossible to remove your fabric. Check your manual for the location of the *needle up/down button or icon*. Simply touch the needle up/down button near the take-up lever, or the image on the touch screen, and instantly the needle moves to its highest position.

Tie off stitch button or touch screen icon

Newer sewing machines come equipped with a *tie off* stitch feature. The machine sews several stitches right on top of its self. Now your seam will not come unraveled. You will find this button located above the needle or the image on the touch screen. Check your manual under "tie off".

Mirror Image button or touch screen icon

WOW! This is great. When sewing a centered zipper the *mirror image* button allows you a precise needle placement to sew a straight seam just the right distance from the zipper teeth. Remember to start sewing from the bottom of the zipper and sew up on both sides. But what about the decorative stitches? (Example: the heart can be mirrored: △♡△♡△well, you get the idea.) What a nice feature. Have fun with this one.

You have unlocked the mystery *of your sewing machines* magical powers!

PATTERN INSTRUCTIONS

Burda pattern instruction sheets are sometimes difficult to read because of the intricate designs. Vogue is a close second. Therefore let's avoid them until you get to the more advanced stage of your sewing lessons. In the mean time I will attempt to clear up some of the more confusing instructions. Would you believe it is as simple as reading every word? It's true! Study this book as you go through the instructions and you will get it!

Hummmmm, Vogue pattern instructions, you got to love 'um!

THE PATTERN ENVELOPE

~~~Front of envelope~~~
~~~Areas to look at when purchasing a pattern~~~
(for woven fabrics)

1.   Check to make sure you have: a) the right design (is the lapel to large for you?) and b) the correct size. On this pattern it is in the lower left corner.

2.   Look carefully at the design (an actual photo on a model well give you a better idea how the design will ware). Drawings are nice when viewing details, but sometimes the design can be misleading. When I purchased this pattern I did not take into consideration how wide the collar is on the real model. For me my shoulders are to narrow to ware such a wide collar.

3.   Check the view letter, this pattern envelope indicates that **B** is for long sleeves. If you want short sleeves, **A** is the view for you. Knowing this you will not be tempted to purchase too much or too little fabric. Also this knowledge will help you cut out only the pattern pieces you will need. So many times my students (and me on occasion) waist time by cutting out pattern pieces printed on tissue paper that are not part of the view style chosen. "Oh Bother" (See explanation on page 29)

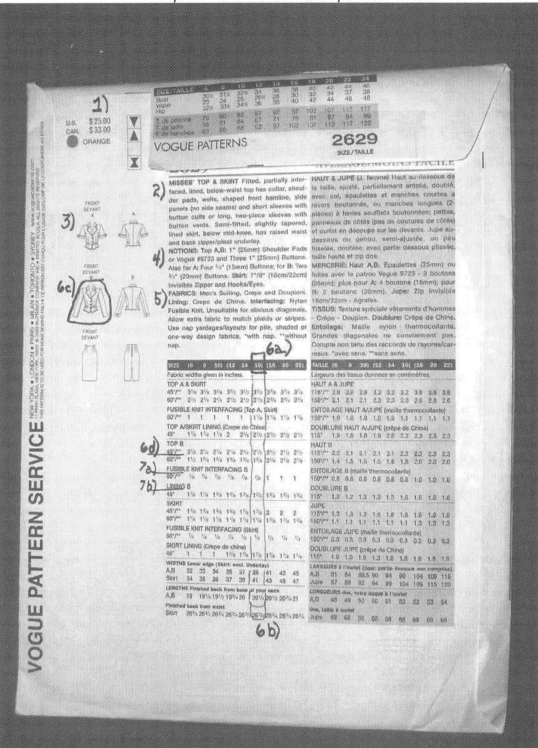

~~~Back of envelope~~~
~~~Areas to look at when purchasing the pattern/fabric/notions~~~
(for woven fabric)

1)   Check the price. Vogue is notorious for printing expensive patterns. I especially enjoy making the Vogue designs so I allow for the increase in cost. Of course, this is a mater of preference.

2)   Read the <u>description</u> carefully so you know what you are getting yourself into.

3)   Study the details in the drawings of the front and back views. See the darkened line on the skirt? This indicates the placement for a zipper. If a dark line is located at the side this could mean a pocket is sewed in the side seam. Note any button placements, collar details, etc.

4)   Notions: It is best to collect all the notions when you purchase your fabrics. You may need to preshrink ribbons or tailors tape, et cetera.

5)   Fabrics: This pattern suggests Doupioni. You might check the price before you get your heart set on Doupioni fabric. It is usually higher priced then other fabrics. With NAP means the fabric has a pile (think velvet) which lays down in one direction and stands up in the opposite direction. This changes the color some what. More fabric is required because all the pattern pieces need to be pinned going the same direction. In-other-words, you should not place the hem of the <u>center back</u> pattern piece up against the hem of the <u>side back</u> pattern piece: unless you desire this color change. When pinning, be sure you align the *grain line* with the selvage edge. Until you gain confidence in your sewing ability you may want to hold off sewing velvet, satin and sequined fabrics.

6)   Fabric Required: Some pattern envelopes have the size chart printed on the flap. Note your size by checking the bust, waist, and hip measurements. Have another person take your measurements, because you can not be accurate on yourself. I like to circle the size (6a). Now draw a rectangle below your size (6b). This will help you identify the yardage needed for your size. Keep in mind which garment you have chosen, 6c. After determining how wide your fabric is, run your left forefinger across the envelope and your right forefinger down from your size (6d). Where your fingers meet indicates the amount of fabric you will need.

7)   Note any interfacing (7a) and lining (7b) required.

8)   Now you have to choose our fabrics/linings/interfacings/trims, "Good Grief", this is a process you do not want to rush. After collecting everything you like, your next stop is the cutting table. Because you have taken the time to study the back of your Pattern Envelope, the person cutting your fabric will appreciate your preparation. A very satisfying experience for the both of you! And, the other shoppers in line behind you will be grateful for your quickness in ordering your fabric. Good Job!

Sample of Pattern Envelope Front (using knit or Spandex fabrics, only)

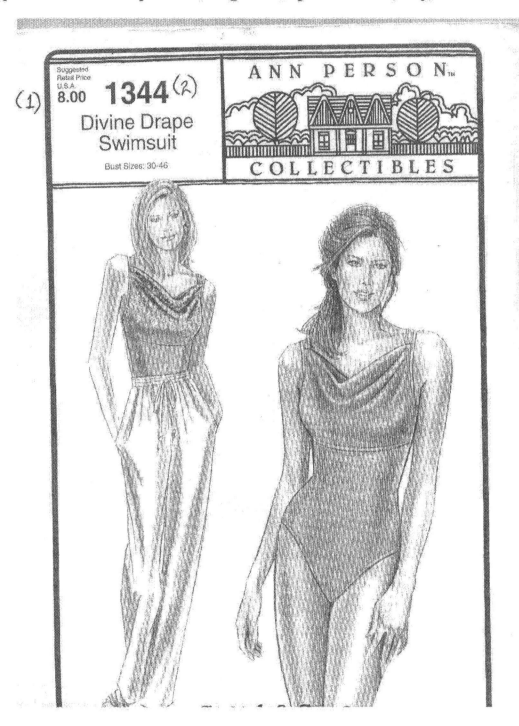

Suggested Retail Price U.S.A 8.00

(1)

1344 (2)

Divine Drape Swimsuit

Bust Sizes: 30-46

ANN PERSON™

COLLECTIBLES

~~~Front of envelope~~~
~~~Areas to look at when purchasing a pattern~~~
(for knits, Spandex, and stretch woven fabrics)

1)   Note the price (some fabric stores are selling the Pattern's for 40 – 50% off). This will help to ease your sewing budget. I remember when patterns cost 35 cents. Jeez Louise!

2)   Make sure you choose the Pattern you want by checking the Pattern Number. And, I recommend you study the design. I would not have chosen this one if I had relied on the drawing with the French leg style. However, a quick read of the description on the back panel tells a different story. So, I purchased it and made the lower cut leg style. How smart we can be when we have a better understanding of the whole sewing experience.

Notes:

Sample of Pattern Envelope Back (using knit or Spandex fabrics, only)

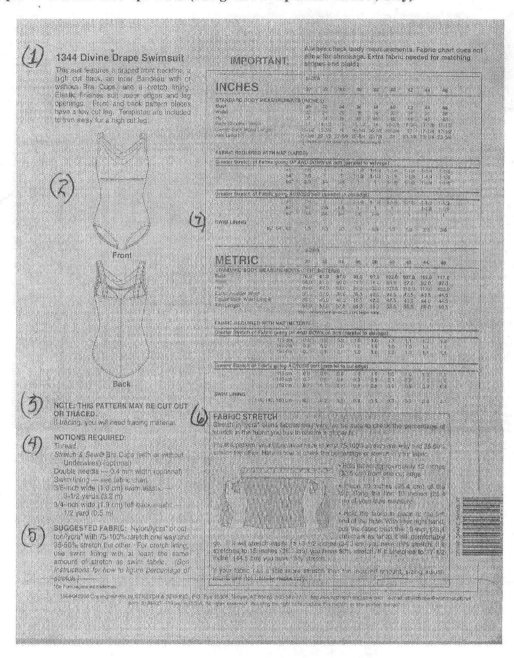

~~~Back of envelope~~~
~~~Areas to look at when purchasing a pattern/fabrics/notions~~~
(for knit, Spandex and stretch woven fabrics)

1)   Read the description to make sure this is the Pattern for you.

2)   Study the Front & Back views, there might be a detail you hadn't planned on making.

3)   <u>Note: This Pattern may be cut out or traced</u>. In-other-words, this Pattern Company prints on heavier paper – not tissue. The heavy paper is difficult to pin to fabric, especially light weight knits. Allow time to trace the Pattern on lighter paper or muslin. Speaking of muslin, this makes excellent patterns should you want to make several garments of this design.

4)   Notions Required: After you have chosen your Pattern you need to collect all the notions printed on the back side of the envelope. I recommend use the special cotton elastic made for swimwear and special *Stretch & Sew* bra cups. If your teacher is experienced in sewing swim ware she can help you assemble all these special notions.

5)   Suggested Fabrics: Take note, this design is to hug your figure, not allowing any ease in the fabric. If you should purchase non stretch woven fabrics you will run the risk of the seams popping out, not a good idea when you plunge into the public pool!

6)   I suggest reading the *Fabric Stretch* section to determine which *Greater Stretch* you prefer. Next, run your fingers straight down the envelope. Note the width measurement of the fabric you wish to purchase. (Ex: most Spandex fabrics are between 58" to 60" wide selvage to selvage. Some knit fabrics have glue at the selvage to keep it from fraying: be sure to place your pattern inside these selvages.) Now run your finger across to you size. This will tell you how much fabric is required.

7)   Note any lining and interfacing required. I like to purchase swim ware knit lining, comes in a couple of flush tones.

8)   Now you are ready to take your fabric to the cutting table. With your newly found information you can order what is required and sound like you have been doing this for years. Knowledge is empowering!

My friends at Yardage Town
Vista, CA

Where I taught sewing
Oceanside, CA

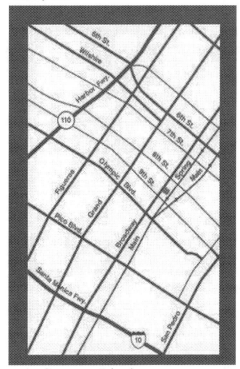

L.A. Garment District

Sew Creative Costume Academy
Temecula, CA

A couple of periodicals

Sewing Sisters Quilt Shop
Carlsbad, CA
(Alas, this store recently closed.)

#18 Reading the pattern instructions gives me a headache

Drawing 18-1

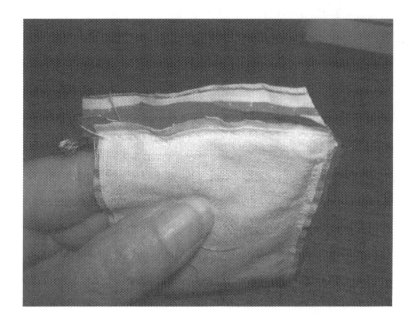

Photo 18-2

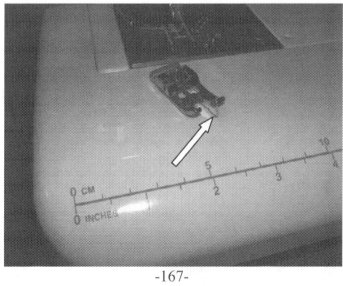

(18-1) Tendency..."It says here to trim and grade the SA, seam allowances. What's that?"
The Problem.......When the SA is <u>not</u> trimmed and graded, it will create an unsightly bump on the outside of the garment. After ironing the garment several times this bump will start to shine.
To Clarify...........Some times you can't avoid a bulky SA. There are at least two layers of fabric in the seam area. At the cuff there can be six layers in the seam area. Trimming and grading to the rescue. The SA closest to the garments outside fabric can be left untrimmed. Each seceding SA gets trimmed gradually, cutting them narrower and narrower, (see Photo 18-1). Be sure not to trim the last SA to close: some woven fabrics can unravel causing the fabric to disappear at the seam. Here is one method that works for me: 1) sew the collar onto the bodice; 2) press seam flat; 3) allow the SA closest to the bodice to remain uncut; 4) cut the next SA a little shorter then the last SA. Now you can press the SA towards the collar. Good! You have successfully graded your SA. Now! Take a moment and step away from your sewing/serging machine. Do some stretches: arms, legs, back and hands (spread fingers apart). Even message your ears with your finger tips (this courtesy of Robin Gladish, my soft Yoga instructor). This can help you stay more alert. Can you feel the tension fading away?
<u>A rule of thumb: the interfacing SA should be cut the closest to the seam. When sewing with iron-on interfacing I trim all the way around ½" before pressing the interfacing on to the fashion fabric: glue side down, please, on wrong side (ugly side) of fashion fabric.</u>

(18-2) Tendency...What is the difference between *top stitching* and *edge stitching*?
The Problem.......Top stitching! This takes too much time and, did you say I have to sew in a straight line? NO STRESS HERE! Why should you care? Well, sharp skirt pleats will sag and casual pants creases in the front fade after washing. So you need to top stitch.
To Clarify...........Top stitching is sewed through two fabric layers and edge stitching usually three. Your garment will take on a really nice quality. Everyone will want to know where you bought it: which will cheer you on to say something like, "I made it myself!" Top stitching can make your clothes sing! One way to show off your skills is to top stitch using decorative stitches. Use contrasting colored thread for more detail. The top stitching around collars, pocket flaps and lapels are usually stitched about ¼ to 3/8" from the edge. The stitch length can be long. Pearl Cotton, found in the thread display or yarn area of your favorite fabric store is excellent for top stitching. Use a *top stitch needle*; it has a larger eye for ease of threading. To make permanent pleated skirts, use the edge stitching technique. First press the crease <u>on the grain line</u> then sew a seam 1/16" from folded edge from waist to hip line. Pull top thread to underside and tie them off. Finish with The Legend of the Disappearing thread technique on page 34. Edge stitching is nice for casual pants to help create a precise crease on the front. A tool that will help you sew a straight seam is the edge stitching foot. (Photo 18-2 see arrow pointing to the vertical flange) A sewing teacher can demonstrate the eye-hand-foot technique. See what you can aspire to? Practice sewing on lined paper and you will be able to sew a straight line in no time. Be sure to purchase the foot that fits your machine – remember to have the make of your machine and either model # or the type of foot shank: high shank; low shank or slant needle. Measure from center of the foot screw down to the surface of machine: high = 1", low = 1/2". The generic feet can fit many sewing machines on the market. Quilting a garment creates a special fascination for the observer. It's a WOW factor! A pattern or meandering stitch (common in quilting, use a *quilting needle*) holds at least three layers of fabric together over a large area giving it a raised effect. The feet for the *Bernina* machines are totally unique and work fabulously.

Photo 18-3

Drawing 18-4

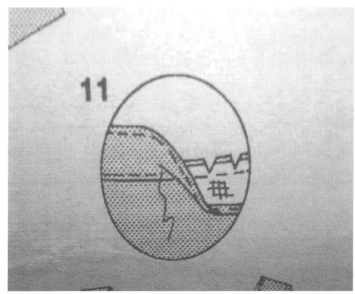

(18-3) Tendency...I see students cramming their pattern pieces into the envelope. Yuck!

The Problem.......A common problem: say you need to check something on that one piece you stuffed in the envelope or you only cut 2 when you needed 4. Finding the piece will result in time wasted searching through the tangled mess and the necessity, once you find it, to repress the paper flat so you can use it, again. More time wasted!

To Clarify...........I have a better way. As soon as you lift the pattern piece off the fabric and you are satisfied you have marked everything properly, lay the paper face down on the table. First carefully fold any curves or points inside. Next, start folding all four sides inward. Press lightly, with a flat hand, as you fold. The goal is to make a neat package. Turn over the package, you should see: the pattern number (ex: 2); what piece it is (ex: Front bodice), and the pattern company name (ex: New Look). This takes a short amount of time compared to rifling through the scrunched up paper patterns. And believe it or not all the pattern pieces will fit inside the envelope without splitting its sides. [I bet dollars to donuts during your sewing career you will probably need to check several pattern pieces for that detail you neglected to mark.] After each pattern piece is folded, wrap the instruction sheet(s) around the folded bundle. Easing the paper pattern bundle into the envelope will be a breeze. I don't know about you, the seasoned seam stress, but I have lost pattern pieces before I developed this system of management. Now I have time to do more sewing! Whooppeeeee!

(18-4) Tendency..."*Understitch*! Why do I have to *understitch*? "

The Problem........*Understitching* is often not done. If you do not understitch the facing it will poke out, messing up the purpose of sewing the facings to finish the neck edge.

To Clarify...........(Drawing 18-4) Here is the deal: 1) stitch the neck facing to the bodice; 2) grade the SA; 3) clip the SA; 4) press the SA flat; 5) on the inside press the SA towards the facing. In the curved areas use the pressing ham (see Tendency 12-3 page 104). Mean while back at the sewing machine: place the bodice and facing, "pretty side" up, under the foot next to the seam line. Be sure to have the facing to the right of the needle. The needle will pierce the facing (facing and two SA s), on the "pretty side" of the facing just 1/16" from seam line. Stitch slowly because you are sewing in a tight curve. When understitching on a straight line you can go some what faster, but not to fast. Use a long stitch (4-6) on the dial: depending on your particular controls. This technique will pull the seam towards the underside and out of sight, like magic!

Drawing 18-5

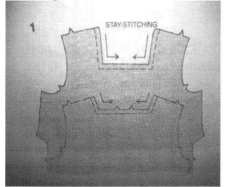

Photo 18-5a

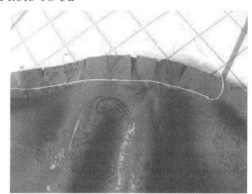

Photo 18-5b

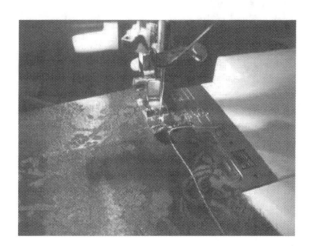

(18-5) Tendency...What is *stay-stitching*; and why do I need it? What is with the arrows on the instruction sheet? (Drawing 18-5)

The Problem.......When fabric is cut in a curve to accommodate the neck, the fabric has the potential to stretch out of shape. If you *Stay-stitch* the neck opening continuously from one end to the other this will cause half of the neck to stretch out of shape. There is more to stay stitching then randomly placing the fabric under the foot.

To Clarify...........On the pattern instruction, the arrows indicate the direction the *stay-stitching* is to be sewn. Start sewing at the shoulder edge of the neck opening and stop at center front or back. Use a standard stitch length between 2 for lighter weight fabric and 3 for heavier weight fabric. Test your sewing machine for the effect you want. Cut a short thread tail, then <u>turn the piece over</u> and start at the other shoulder sewing to the center stopping just as you reach the end of the first *stay-stitching*: no need to overlap. (Photo 18-5b) When constructing a Princess style bodice, the instructions tell you to *stay stitch* the side front and side back section between triangular marks or dots (Photo 18-5a). Next clip the SA up to the *stay-stitching*. For the satin brocade fabric I shorten the *stay-stitching* stitch length to about a one on the dial, helps protect the fabric from ripping due to its tendency to ravel easily.
Special note about stitching shoulder seams: The direction in which you sew seams is important. Shoulder seams are cut at an angle: should you start the seam from the sleeve sewing towards the neck edge you will run the risk of stretching the fabric. Therefore start at the neck edge. The same goes for skirts where the fabric curves near the waist. Start at the bottom edge and sew up. The seam will lie smooth with out stretching.

Notes:

Appendix

Index

"Oh, Bother", said Winnie the Pooh, I nearly forgot:

You know that strawberry attached to your *tomato pin cushion*? My young students today call it the "*little chili*". What ever you call it, do not put pins in it. Instead, use the strawberry to clean your *hand sewing needles.* After a while the oils in your fingers corrode the needle making it almost impossible to push the needle through the fabric. (One of my new students brought in her daughters Halloween costume because she was having problems sewing a decent hem. I had to laugh at her *pin cushion.* Her children stuck more pins in the strawberry than in the tomato.) Should you be tempted to sharpen your needle, do not bother. When hand or machine needles get dull, send them to *needle heaven* (the trash) and resume sewing with a new and fresh needle. You will find your sewing to be smoother and avoid the possibility of snagging your fabric. Keep in mind, the thread will not snag with a fresh needle.

In the newer sewing machines one will probably find this funny looking thing. Believe it or not, this is a screwdriver. Ordinary screwdrivers are long and can not fit under the needle/foot shaft housing unit making them exceedingly clumsy when attempting to loosen the throat plate screws in the feed teeth area. Removing the throat plate allows easy access for cleaning which should be done immediately after sewing fabrics like fleece. A couple of times I have seen the feed dogs so impacted with lint that they would not move. Wow! That is ill maintained sewing machine. Now you can understand the phrase, "Preventive maintenance". I found another benefit for this funny looking thing: I was putting together a bathroom shelving unit and realized my regular screwdriver was too long to get into a tiny space. As I struggled, I remembered my funny looking screwdriver. It worked. I didn't have to take a wall out just to tighten a screw. Smashing! No pun intended.

About Stephnie

Stephnie Clark has been sewing so long; she believes she was born with a thimble on her middle finger. The summer before her senior year at Orange High School, Orange, CA, she sewed enough to have a complete change of garment for the first three months of classes. That is a plethora of garments.

In the 60's Stephnie Clark sold Singer sewing machines, Torrance, CA. The 70's she sold fabric and notions at the Singer store and taught beginning through tailoring for students age 10 thru 16 as part of the summer program, in Honolulu, Hawaii. Five of Stephnie's students entered the Hawaii State Singer Sewing contest and all five were in the top three positions, including two of the first place winners. For the past nine years, Stephnie Clark as been teaching beginning sewing through tailoring in San Diego North County, CA. Stephnie is a Grandmother of three, and a former; Phi Theta Kappa member, Vice President of Alpha Xi Phi chapter; bass singer for Sweet Adeline's Marin County, CA and Olympia, WA choirs'; Habitat for Humanity architectural drafter and board member, Olympia, WA; docent for the California Historical society, San Francisco, CA; continual contributor to the ONE DRESS AT A TIME organization; and attended the Costume College in Van Nuys, CA, summer of 2005 (what a hoot!) In 2002 and 2003 she directed two fashion shows. Stephnie is enjoying retirement and the balmy breezes in Oceanside, CA. However, she is eager to push retirement aside and get back in the game of spreading the magic of sewing.

Printed in the United States
by Baker & Taylor Publisher Services